Easy DOS,®
Second Edition

Shelley O'Hara

Easy DOS,® Second Edition

Library of Congress Catalog No.: 93-83033

ISBN 1-56529-095-X

95 94 93 6 5 4 3 2

Interpretation of the printing code: the rightmost double-digit number is the year of the book's printing; the rightmost single-digit number, the number of the book's printing. For example, a printing code of 93-1 shows that the first printing of the book occurred in 1993.

Screen reproductions in this book were created using Collage Plus from Inner Media, Inc., Hollis, NH.

Easy DOS is based on MS-DOS Version 6.0.

Publisher: Lloyd J. Short

Associate Publisher: Rick Ranucci

Operations Manager: Sheila Cunningham

Book Design: Scott Cook

Production Team: Claudia Bell, Julie Brown, Jodie Cantwell, Laurie Casey, Michelle Cleary, Mark Enochs, John Kane, Jay Lesandrini, Tim Montgomery, Caroline Roop, Tina Trettin, Phil Worthington

Production Editor
Cindy Morrow

Technical Editor
David Knispel

Novice Reviewer
Melissa Keegan

About the Author

Shelley O'Hara is a Title Manager at Que Corporation. She is the author of 17 books in the Easy series, including the bestselling *Easy WordPerfect*, *Easy Windows*, and *Easy 1-2-3*. She is also the coauthor of *Real Men Use DOS*. Ms. O'Hara received her bachelors degree from the University of South Carolina and her masters degree from the University of Maryland.

Introduction

What Is DOS?

With a personal computer, you can type professional-looking letters, draw a map to your house, create letterhead, balance your checkbook, create charts, inquire about stock prices, play games, do homework, learn to type, and so on, and so on.

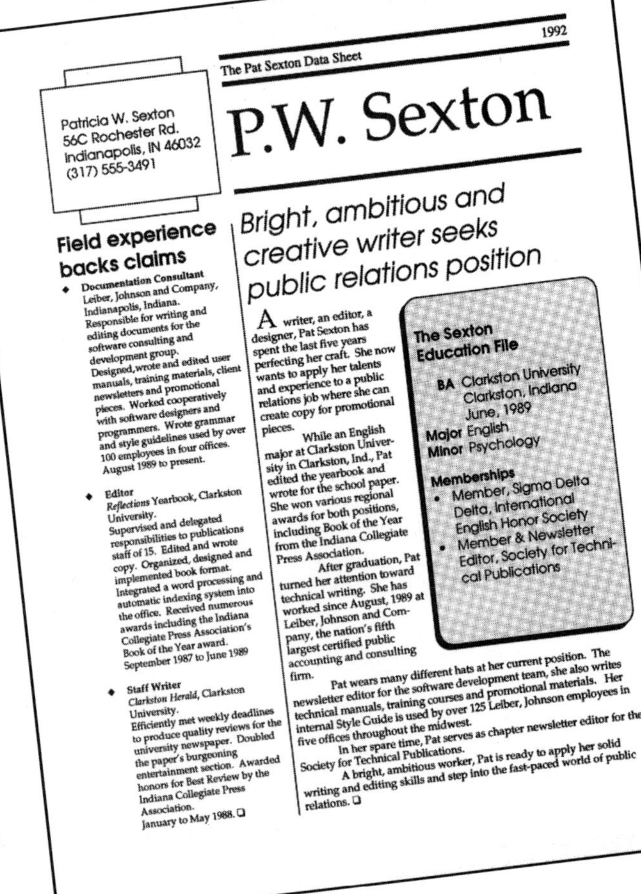

1992

The Pat Sexton Data Sheet

P.W. Sexton

Patricia W. Sexton
56C Rochester Rd.
Indianapolis, IN 46032
(317) 555-3491

Field experience backs claims

- **Documentation Consultant**
Leiber, Johnson and Company, Indianapolis, Indiana.
Responsible for writing and editing documents for the software consulting and development group.
Designed,wrote and edited user manuals, training materials, client newsletters and promotional pieces. Worked cooperatively with software designers and programmers. Wrote grammar and style guidelines used by over 100 employees in four offices.
August 1989 to present.

- **Editor**
Reflections Yearbook, Clarkston University.
Supervised and delegated responsibilities to publications staff of 15. Edited and wrote copy. Organized, designed and implemented book format.
Integrated a word processing and automatic indexing system into the office. Received numerous awards including the Indiana Collegiate Press Association's Book of the Year award.
September 1987 to June 1989

- **Staff Writer**
Clarkston Herald, Clarkston University.
Efficiently met weekly deadlines to produce quality reviews for the university newspaper. Doubled the paper's burgeoning entertainment section. Awarded honors for Best Review by the Indiana Collegiate Press Association.
January to May 1988. ❑

Bright, ambitious and creative writer seeks public relations position

A writer, an editor, a designer, Pat Sexton has spent the last five years perfecting her craft. She now wants to apply her talents and experience to a public relations job where she can create copy for promotional pieces.

While an English major at Clarkston University in Clarkston, Ind., Pat edited the yearbook and wrote for the school paper. She won various regional awards for both positions, including Book of the Year from the Indiana Collegiate Press Association.

After graduation, Pat turned her attention toward technical writing. She has worked since August, 1989 at Leiber, Johnson and Company, the nation's fifth largest certified public accounting and consulting firm.

Pat wears many different hats at her current position. The newsletter editor for the software development team, she also writes technical manuals, training courses and promotional materials. Her internal Style Guide is used by over 125 Leiber, Johnson employees in five offices throughout the midwest.

In her spare time, Pat serves as chapter newsletter editor for the Society for Technical Publications.

A bright, ambitious worker, Pat is ready to apply her solid writing and editing skills and step into the fast-paced world of public relations. ❑

The Sexton Education File

BA Clarkston University
Clarkston, Indiana
June, 1989

Major English
Minor Psychology

Memberships

- Member, Sigma Delta Delta, International English Honor Society
- Member & Newsletter Editor, Society for Technical Publications

To do anything on a personal computer, you need:

- Hardware
- Software
- An operating system

Hardware is the actual machine—keyboard, monitor, and system unit. Hardware refers to the items that you can see and touch.

Software refers to the programs that you run on the hardware. The words *program*, *application*, and *software* are all used interchangeably. Sometimes the terms are combined: application program, software application. They all mean the same thing.

You're cordially invited to the grand opening of our new store in Greenwood. Grab a friend, load the Winnebego, and head out to receive fabulous savings on every kind of tome your heart desires. We have it all—classics, biography, fine literature, how-to, art, technical...everything! Bring in this invitation for a 10 percent discount on every regular-priced book you purchase.

Captain Ahab Books

3901 Breaker—In the Greenwood Plaza

Think of a program as a specialist hired to perform a task. You might need an accountant to plan your budget and calculate your taxes, a typist to do mailings, an artist to create a logo, a stockbroker to quote stock prices, and so on. Rather than have a specialist, you have a program. For accounting tasks, you might use a spreadsheet program. For typing letters, you would use a word processor. You would use a drawing program to create maps and logos. Each of these programs runs on the personal computer.

The operating system is the link between the hardware and the software. The operating system, called DOS (disk operating system), manages files and runs programs.

You cannot accomplish anything without DOS. The computer and programs are useless. With DOS itself, you can do some things (copy files, for instance). When you add programs, however, you can do all kinds of things (as previously described).

MEMORANDUM

TO: All Employees
FROM: Melissa Lowery
DATE: December 29, 1991

RE: New In-House Illustrator

I am pleased to announce that Susan Trautman has recently joined our staff as an in-house illustrator.

For the past two years, Susan has been working as a free-lance illustrator, and her outstanding drawings have enhanced several of our best-selling children's books. Most recently, Susan's work has graced *Peter Goes to the Salad Bar* and *Zachary Meets the Baby Sitter*.

Susan's experience includes over a decade of illustration and layout experience in both the publishing and advertising fields. We are all excited about the possibilities opened to us by bringing Ms. Trautman on our staff full-time.

Please join me in welcoming Susan to the McBryer Publishing staff.

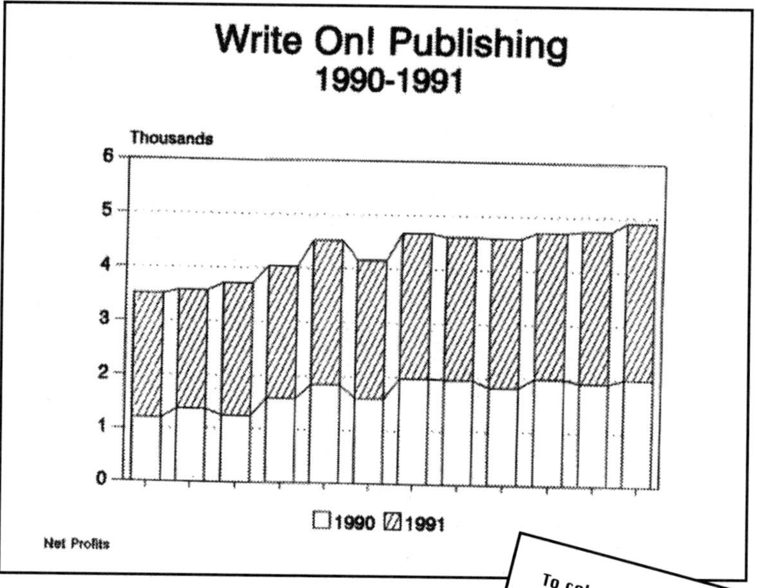

Two of the basic things DOS does are

Start programs. To start and use a program, you first start the computer. Then you type the appropriate command to start the program.

Manage files. Applications create *files*. A letter, a budget, and a mailing list are all separate files. You use DOS to display files, copy files, move files, rename files, and perform other file-management tasks.

To celebrate our new home, we (Reggie and are inviting you to the party of the decade. the decade of the 70s, that is. Yes, come one come all, come in your track shorts and tube socks, come in your three-piece white suit an gold chains, come in your powder blue polyest prom dress. It's the first official 70s bash, and we want you there.

- Thrill to dancing cheek-to-cheek to such classic love songs as Samantha Sang's "Emotion" and Andy Gibb's "I Just Want to Be Your Everything."
- Get down and boogie to the best in dance music with the BeeGees, the Commodores, and K.C. & the Sunshine Band.
- Relax and unwind while watching a screening of the Academy Award nominee of 1977, Saturday Night Fever.
- Enter the first official hustle and disco contest and walk away with our grand prize zodiac medallion.

Hope to see you there. We'll keep a lava light on for you.

Date: February 11

Place: Reggie and Val's pad (2414 Seymour Lake Road)

Time: 8:00 until the last pair of boogie shoes leaves the dance floor.

Why You Need This Book

DOS is not easy to learn. You must memorize commands, and you must type the commands in an exact format (called the *syntax* of the command). DOS doesn't give you any clues about how to proceed. You only see a small prompt (`C:\>`, for instance). To use programs, you MUST learn some basic DOS commands.

But don't worry. This book is designed to make learning DOS *easy*. This book helps the beginning DOS user perform basic operations. You don't need to worry that your knowledge of computers is limited. This book teaches you all you need to know for basic operations.

You don't need to worry that you might do something wrong and ruin a program or the computer. This book points out mistakes you might make and shows you how to avoid them. This book explains what to do when you change your mind—how to escape from a situation.

Reading this book will build your confidence. It will show you what steps are necessary to get a particular job done.

Remember: DOS does only what you tell it to do. Don't tell it to delete a file unless you would do the same thing manually (that is, send the only remaining copy of that file through a shredder).

How This Book Is Organized

This book is designed with you, the beginner, in mind. The book is divided into several parts:

- Introduction
- The Basics
- Task/Review
- Reference

This Introduction explains how the book is set up and how to use the book.

The next part, The Basics, outlines general information about your computer and its keyboard layout. This part explains basic terms and concepts.

The main part of this book, Task/Review, tells you how to perform a particular task. The first task explains how to start DOS.

The Reference Guide includes a quick reference list of the most common DOS commands, a guide to error messages, a software guide that defines the different application programs you can use on the computer, and a glossary of common computer terms.

How To Use This Book

This book is set up so that you can use it several different ways:

- You can read the book from start to finish, or you can start reading at any point in the book.
- You can experiment with one exercise, many exercises, or all exercises.

- You can look up specific tasks that you want to accomplish, such as displaying a file listing.
- You can flip through the book, looking at the Before and After screens, to find specific tasks.
- You can look at the alphabetical listing of tasks at the beginning of the Task/Review part to find the task you want.
- You can read just the task, just the review, or both the task and review parts. As you learn the program, you might want to follow along with the tasks. After you learn the program, you can use the review part to remind yourself how to perform a certain task.
- You can read any part of the exercises you want. You can read all the text to see both the steps to follow and the explanation of the steps. You can read just the text in red to see only the actions to perform. You can read just the explanation to understand what happens during a particular step.

As you read, don't worry about making a mistake. For many tasks, the book explains how to undo the task. The book also points out errors that you might make and how to avoid them.

Task section

The Task section includes numbered steps that tell you how to accomplish certain tasks, such as copying a file. The numbered steps walk you through a specific example so that you can learn the task by doing it. Blue text below the numbered steps explains the concept in more detail.

Oops! notes

You may find that you have performed a task that you do not want after all. The Oops! notes tell you how to undo each procedure or explain how to get out of a situation. By showing you how to reverse nearly every procedure, these notes enable you to use DOS more confidently.

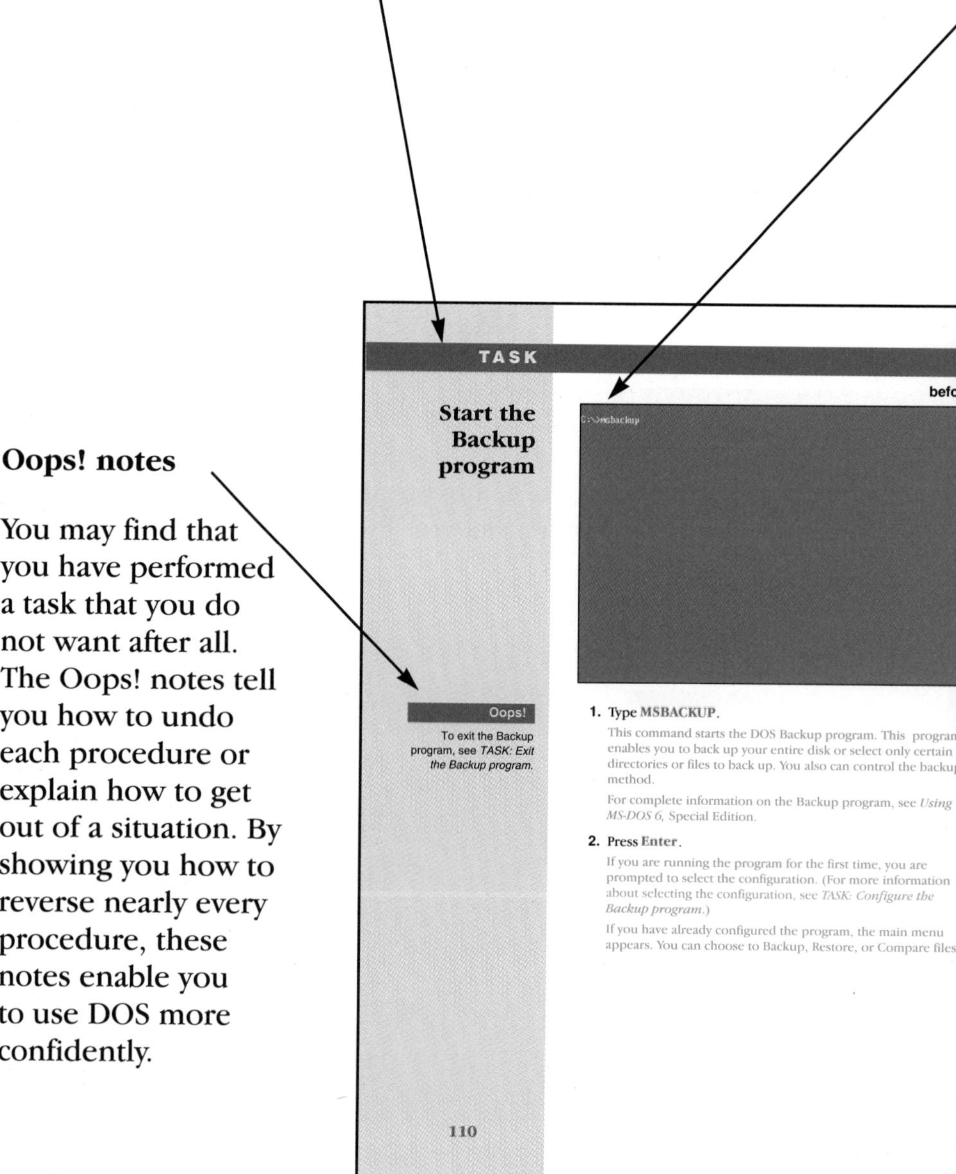

TASK
befo
Start the Backup program
C:\>msbackup
Oops!
To exit the Backup program, see TASK: Exit the Backup program.
1. Type MSBACKUP.
This command starts the DOS Backup program. This program enables you to back up your entire disk or select only certain directories or files to back up. You also can control the backup method.
For complete information on the Backup program, see Using MS-DOS 6, Special Edition.
2. Press Enter.
If you are running the program for the first time, you are prompted to select the configuration. (For more information about selecting the configuration, see TASK: Configure the Backup program.)
If you have already configured the program, the main menu appears. You can choose to Backup, Restore, or Compare files.
110

Before and After screens

Each task includes Before and After screens that show how the computer screen will look before and after you follow the numbered steps in the Task section.

Review section

After you learn a procedure by following a specific example, you can refer to the Review section for a quick summary of the task. The Review section gives you the generic steps for completing a task so that you can apply them to your own work. You can use these steps as a quick reference to refresh your memory about how to perform procedures.

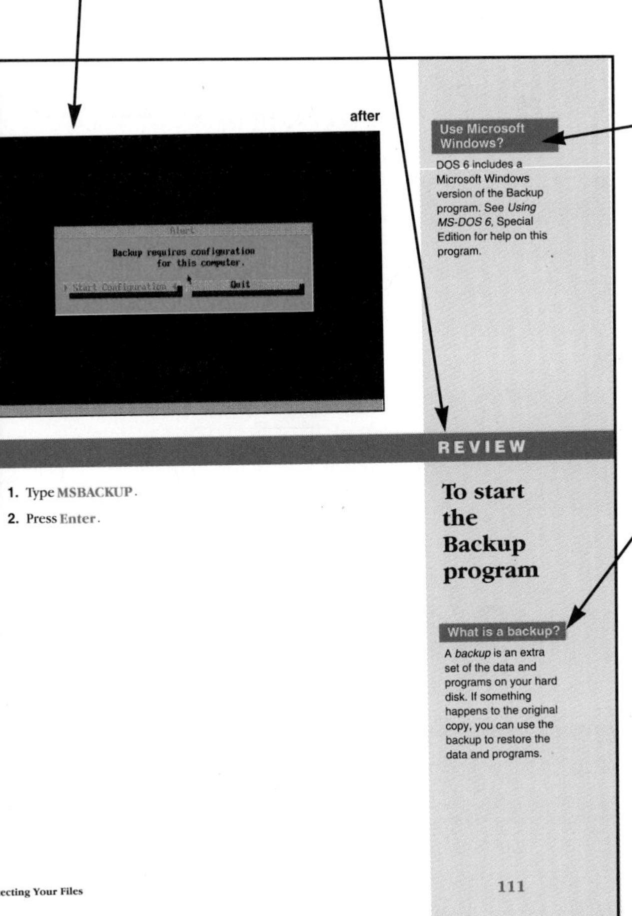

after
Backup requires configuration
for this computer.
Start Configuration
Quit
REVIEW
1. Type MSBACKUP.
2. Press Enter.
To start the Backup program
Use Microsoft Windows?
DOS 6 includes a Microsoft Windows version of the Backup program. See Using MS-DOS 6, Special Edition for help on this program.
What is a backup?
A backup is an extra set of the data and programs on your hard disk. If something happens to the original copy, you can use the backup to restore the data and programs.
111

Other notes

The extra margin notes explain a little more about each procedure. These notes define terms, explain other options, and refer you to other sections, when applicable.

How To Follow an Exercise

For consistency, this book makes certain assumptions about how your computer is set up and how you use DOS. As you follow each exercise, keep the following key points in mind:

- This book assumes that you have a hard drive.
- This book is based on DOS Version 6, but you can use this book with any DOS version. If a particular command is included only in DOS 6, this fact is noted.
- This book mainly covers using DOS from the command prompt. The first part of the Task/Review part covers the command prompt. If you have DOS 5 or 6, you also can use the DOS Shell. The second half of the Task/Review part covers using the DOS Shell to perform some common tasks. This book contains a complete section that covers using the DOS Shell to perform some of the most common tasks.
- This book shows the screens in color. Even if you have a color monitor, however, your screen display will probably appear in black and white.

Where To Get More Help

This book does not cover all DOS commands. This book is geared toward the beginning user—someone who wants just the basics. This person isn't ready for advanced features, such as using the MODE command.

As you become more comfortable, you may need a more complete reference book. Que offers several DOS books to suit your needs:

MS-DOS 6 Quick Reference

MS-DOS 6 QuickStart

Upgrading to MS-DOS 6

Using MS-DOS 6, Special Edition

Que also offers several books on specific software programs. Some of the most popular include the following titles:

Using 1-2-3 Release 2.4, Special Edition

Using Quattro Pro 4, Special Edition

Using WordPerfect 5.1, Special Edition

The following books also will be of interest:

Introduction to Personal Computers, 3rd Edition

Que's Computer User's Dictionary, 3rd Edition

The Basics

Understanding Your Computer System

Using Your Keyboard

Understanding Disk Organization

Typing a Command

Taking Care of the Computer

Understanding Your Computer System

Your computer system is made up of these basic parts:

- The system unit
- The monitor
- The keyboard
- The floppy disk drive(s)
- The hard disk drive

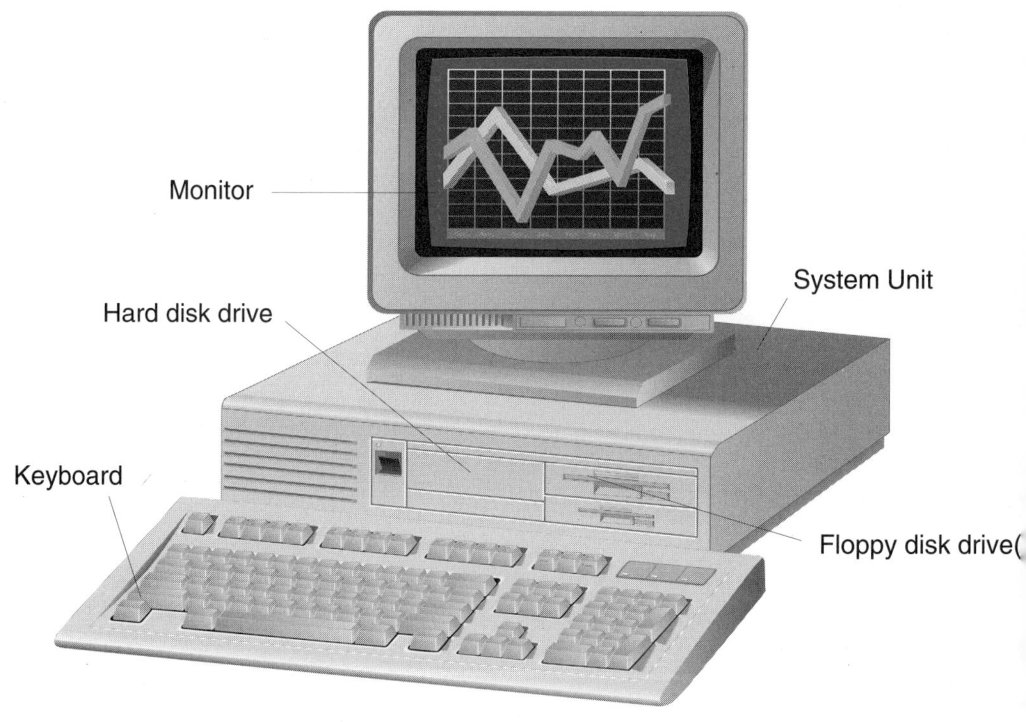

You may also have a mouse and a printer.

System Unit The system unit is the box that holds all the electrical components of your computer. The floppy disk drive and hard disk drive are also usually inside the system unit. (The size of the system unit varies.) Usually the power switch is on the back or side of the box.

Monitor The monitor displays on-screen what you type on the keyboard. Your monitor also may have a power switch.

Keyboard You use the keyboard to communicate with the computer. You use it to type entries and issue commands. You type on the keyboard just as you do on a regular typewriter. A keyboard also has special keys that you use. (Different computers have different keyboards.) These keys are discussed later in the section *Using Your Keyboard*.

Floppy Disk Drive The floppy disk drive is the door into your computer. It allows you to put information on the computer—onto the hard drive—and to take information off the computer—onto a floppy disk.

Hard Disk Drive A hard disk drive stores the programs and files with which you work.

Mouse The mouse is a pointing device that enables you to move the mouse pointer on-screen, select windows, and issue commands.

Printer The printer makes a paper copy (called a "hard copy") of the documents that you create on the computer. To print, you need to attach and install a printer.

More on Floppy Disks

There are two sizes of floppy disks:

- 5 1/4-inch disks
- 3 1/2-inch disks

Your drive uses one size or the other. If you have a 5 1/4-inch drive, use 5 1/4-inch disks. If you have a 3 1/2-inch drive, use 3 1/2-inch disks. Your computer may have two drives—a 5 1/4- and a 3 1/2-inch drive.

Floppy disks differ in size as well as in the amount of information they can store. The amount of information, which is called *capacity*, is measured in kilobytes (abbreviated K) or in megabytes (abbreviated M). One byte equals about one typed character. One kilobyte equals around 1 thousand bytes (1024 to be exact), and one megabyte equals around 1 million bytes.

5 1/4-inch disks come in two capacities: 360K and 1.2M. 360K disks often are called double-density or double-sided double-density (DD). This disk can store around 360,000 characters of information. 1.2M disks often are called double-sided high density (HD). This type of disk can store 1.2 million bytes. (Double-sided means that both sides of the disk store information—like a phonograph record.)

3 1/2-inch disks come in three capacities: 720K, 1.44M, and 2.88M. 720K disks often are called double-density or double-sided double-density (DD). This disk can store around 720,000 characters of information. 1.44M disks often are called double-sided high density (HD). This type of disk can store 1.44 million bytes. The newest floppy size is 2.88M. This disk can store 2.88 million bytes.

The disk drive you have must match the disk type you use. If you have a drive that can "read" only 360K disks, you can only use 360K disks. If you have a drive that can "read" 1.44M disks, then you should use only 1.44M disks. The high-density disk drives (1.2M 5 1/4-inch and 1.44M 3 1/2-inch) can read and write both disk capacities. In general, however, you should use the disk type for your drive.

Disks generally are blank when you purchase them. (A few companies sell preformatted disks.) To prepare a disk for use, you must format it. (See *TASK: Format a disk* in the Task/Review part.) Keep in mind that you must format a disk to the correct capacity. That is, you shouldn't take a 360K disk and format it as a 1.2M disk.

More on Floppy Disk Drives

Your computer has at least one floppy disk drive. You may have more than one. The first floppy disk drive is named drive A, the second, drive B. The hard disk is named drive C.

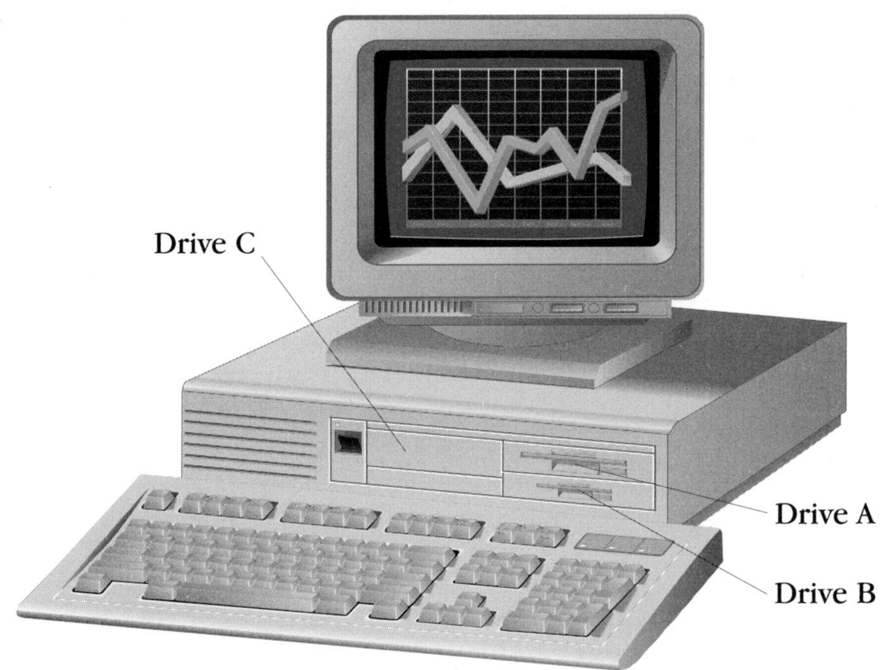

More on Hard Disks

A hard disk is similar to a floppy disk in that it stores information, but a hard disk is much larger and much faster than a floppy disk. A small hard disk might be as much as 25 times larger than a floppy disk. Hard disks are measured in megabytes (M or meg) and come in various sizes: 20M, 30M, 40M, 60M, 80M, 100M, and up.

A hard disk is also hard (rather than floppy) and is usually encased in the system unit. (You also can add an external hard drive.) Some programs require a hard disk, and this book assumes that you have one.

Using Your Keyboard

To communicate with DOS, you type commands at the keyboard. A computer keyboard is just like a typewriter, only a keyboard has additional keys:

- Arrow and other movement keys (Home, PgUp, PgDn, End)
- Function keys (F1-F10 or F1-F12)
- Text editing keys (Backspace, Del, Ins)
- Modifier keys (Shift, Ctrl, Alt)
- Enter
- Other special keys (Print Screen, Scroll Lock, and so on)

For the following keyboard examples, this book uses the Enhanced keyboard. Your keyboard has the same keys, although they might be in a different location. You can familiarize yourself with the keyboard by reading the names on the keys.

These keys are located in different places on different keyboards. For example, sometimes the function keys are across the top of the keyboard. Sometimes they are on the left side of the keyboard.

Different keys perform different actions, depending on the program you are using. In general, the keys perform the following basic functions:

Arrow and other movement keys. In a program, these keys enable you to move around on-screen or select text. Other keys, such as Home, PgUp, PgDn, and End, also move the cursor in programs. (Nothing happens when you press these keys at the DOS prompt.)

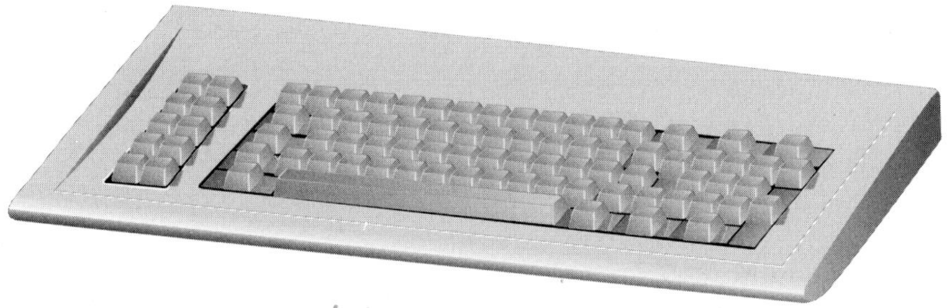

Original PC keyboard

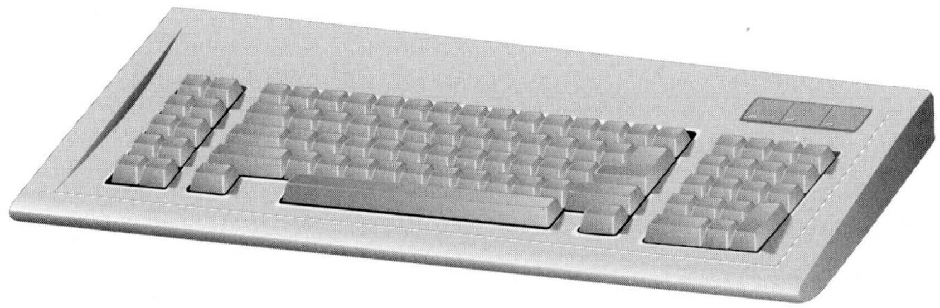

AT keyboard

Enhanced keyboard

Function keys. Function keys initiate commands in programs. The command initiated depends on the program. In WordPerfect, for example, pressing F6 makes text bold.

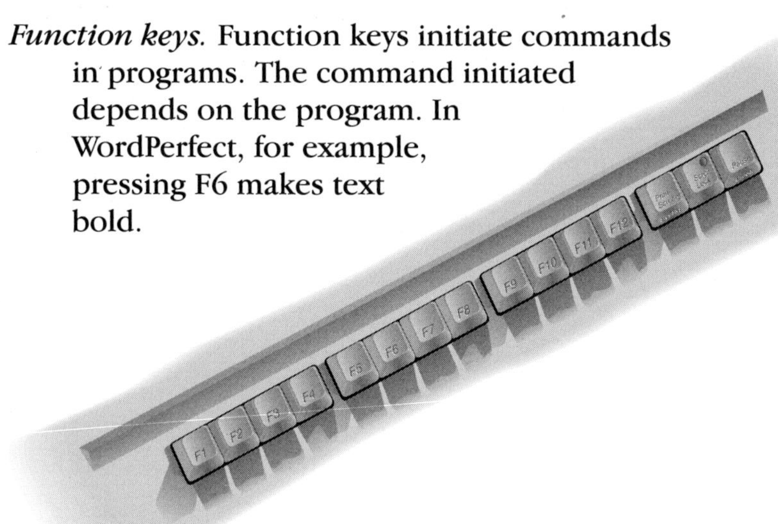

Editing keys (Backspace, Ins, Del). Backspace deletes characters to the left of the cursor. Del works the same way, only it deletes characters at the cursor location and then to the right of the cursor.

Modifier keys (Shift, Ctrl, and Alt). You can use these keys to modify the action of a function key. For example, pressing F6 in WordPerfect tells the program you want to make text bold. Pressing and holding down Shift and then pressing F6 (Shift-F6) tells WordPerfect that you want to center text. The commands assigned to each key and key combination vary from program to program.

Shift also has an additional, more traditional use—it makes lowercase text uppercase (much like on a typewriter).

Enter: This key confirms a command. You also can use it to insert a carriage return when you are typing text.

Understanding Disk Organization

When you first turn on the computer (called "booting" the computer), DOS is loaded or started. (If you want to follow along, turn on the computer. See *TASK: Start DOS* in the Task/Review part.) You see a blank screen with a small prompt. This prompt is intimidating—it offers no clue on what to do next. What's behind that blank screen?

Directories and Files

Think about how you store items in your office. In your office, you may have a filing cabinet. In that filing cabinet, you probably have folders that pertain to different projects, clients, patients, or some other grouping—maybe logical, maybe not. Within each folder you have articles, letters, diagrams, reports—anything that you want to save. This storage method carries over to DOS.

With DOS, a disk is like a filing cabinet. Within that disk, you have directories—areas set aside for certain files (such as memos, articles, or diagrams). The same items that you store in a folder are stored in electronic form in a file. That file is then stored in a directory.

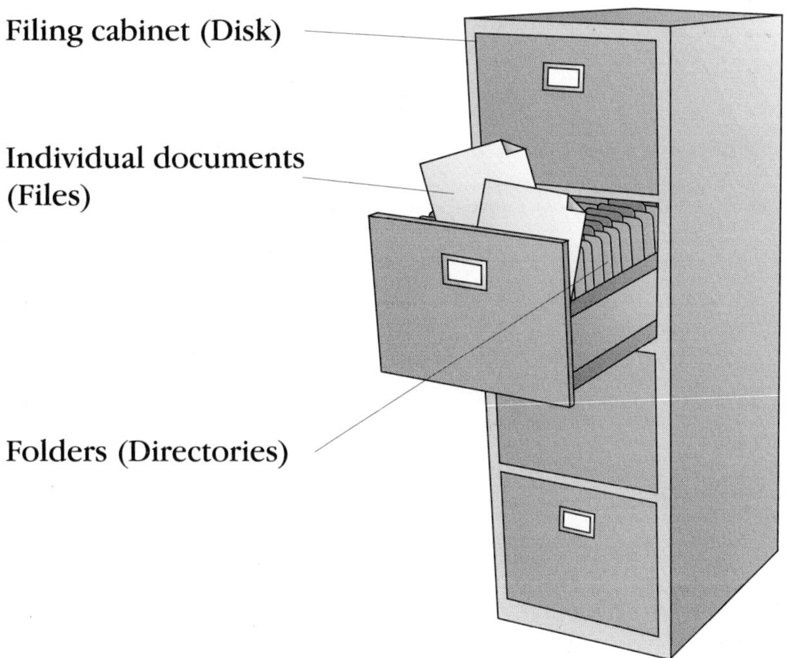

Root Directory and the Path

The main directory is called the root directory. All other directories are branches of this directory, much like the roots of a tree. Directories can contain files, programs, or other directories. The root directory is designated by a backslash (\).

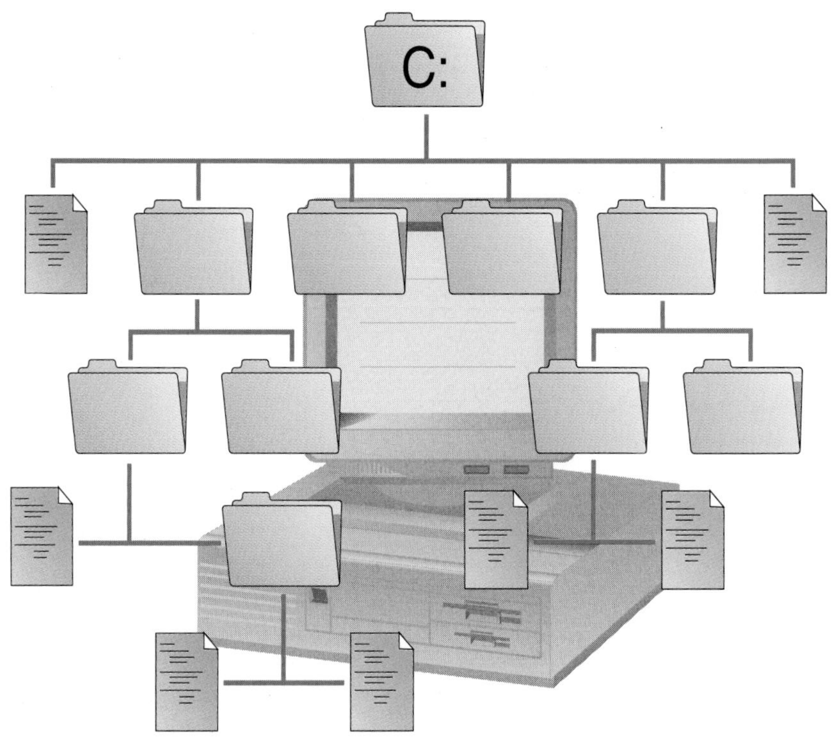

To get to a particular file, you must trace the path from the root directory to the directory that contains the file. The path is the list of directories, starting with the root. Each directory name is separated by a backslash (\). For example, the path

```
C:\WORD\REPORTS
```

gives you these directions: start at drive C, go from the root directory (\) to WORD, and then go to REPORTS.

The structure looks like this:

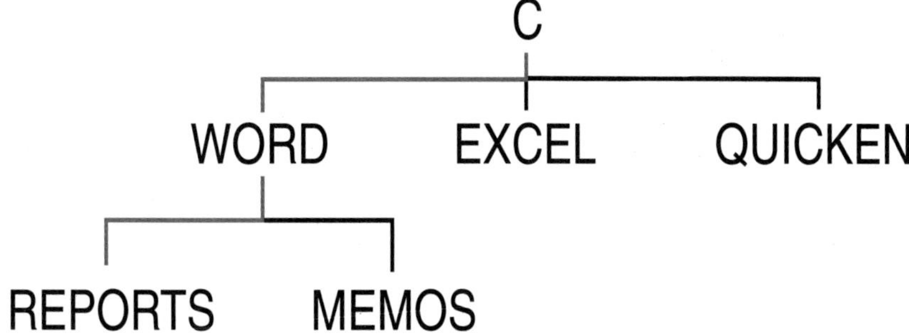

File Names

Each file must have a unique or different name. An entire file name is made up of the file name (up to eight characters) and the extension (optional three characters). The file name and extension are separated by a period. You cannot use these characters in a file name:

" / \ [ ] : ;

REPORT.DOC is a valid file name. REPORT is the file name, and DOC is the extension. The file name should tell you what the report contains; the extension often tells you the type of file. Some programs assign an extension automatically.

MY NOTES is not a valid file name because a file name cannot contain spaces. If you want to include a space in a file name, however, you can use the underline character instead (MY_NOTES).

EASYDOSBOOK.DOC also is not a valid file name because it contains too many characters.

Wild Cards

When you want to work with a group of files, you can use wild cards. There are two types of wild cards: an asterisk and a question mark.

An asterisk wild card (*) matches any characters. The most common use of this wild card is *.*. You might hear other computer users describe this wild card as star-dot-star. This file spec matches all files; that is, the file can have any root name and any extension. (A *file spec* is a combination of the path, file name, and extension.)

The file spec *.TXT specifies files with any root name (*.) and the extension TXT. The following files would be included in this group:

CHAP1.TXT

MEMO.TXT

RESUME.TXT

The following files wouldn't be included (because they have a different extension):

CHAP1.DOC

SALES.XLS

The question mark wild card (?) matches any single character. For instance, the file spec ?SALES.DOC includes all files that start with any character; the remaining letters must be SALES, and the file must have the extension DOC. The following files would be included in this group:

ESALES.DOC

WSALES.DOC

SSALES.DOC

NSALES.DOC

The following files wouldn't be included:

SWSALES.DOC (? matches only one character)

ESALES.XLS (extensions don't match)

You can use wild cards in different combinations to control which files are included in a group.

Suppose, for example, that you are writing a book that has eight chapters. The file for each chapter is named CHAP, followed by the chapter number, a period, and the file extension DOC. When you want to copy all the files (CHAP1.DOC through CHAP8.DOC), you can use a file spec such as

CHAP?.DOC

This file spec uses the ? wild card and tells DOS to include every file named CHAP that is followed by one character and has a DOC extension. Remember that each ? wild card represents one character.

If, however, your book is 15 chapters long, and the files are named CHAP1.DOC through CHAP15.DOC, you need to use a different wild card—the asterisk. To copy all the files for this book, you can use a file spec such as

CHAP*.DOC

This file spec tells DOS to include every file named CHAP, followed by any number of characters, with a DOC extension. Remember that the * wild card represents any number of characters.

Special Files

Your computer contains some special files that you should understand.

To process commands, you must have a file called COMMAND.COM. This is a special DOS file. When you install DOS on a disk, this file is copied to the hard drive.

When you first start DOS, it looks for a file called AUTOEXEC.BAT. This file must be stored in the root directory. When DOS starts and finds the file, it executes the file. This file may include commands that control different settings. For example, you might include a command that tells DOS where your programs are located. This command is called a *path command*.

The following shows a simple AUTOEXEC.BAT file:

```
PROMPT $P$G

PATH C:\DOS;C:\WP51
```

This file changes your prompt (C:\) so that it displays the current subdirectory. For example, if you are in the directory DATA, which is a subdirectory of C:\WP51, you would see

```
C:\WP51\DATA>
```

The PATH command tells DOS to look in the DOS and WP51 directories for program files.

Another special file that DOS uses to start is CONFIG.SYS, a configuration file. Some applications require special commands. These commands are contained in the CONFIG.SYS file.

The following shows a simple CONFIG.SYS file:

```
FILES=20

BUFFERS=25
```

These settings control how DOS uses files. Some programs require that these are set to a certain value.

When dealing with these files, keep these rules in mind:

- Don't delete any of these files: COMMAND.COM, AUTOEXEC.BAT, or CONFIG.SYS.
- Don't try to change the contents of COMMAND.COM.

- As you add applications to the computer, the program manual might tell you to make changes to the AUTOEXEC.BAT file or the CONFIG.SYS file. You must use a special text editor to modify these files. Be careful when making any changes. You should understand each command in the file before changing anything.

DOS Versions

You may have heard DOS called MS-DOS or PC DOS. For all practical purposes, they are the same. DOS is DOS.

DOS is updated periodically: new commands are added, other commands are made to work better, and bugs (problems) are fixed. The most current DOS is Version 6. This book is based on DOS 6.

The Shell

DOS 5 and 6 include a shell. (DOS 4 also had a shell, but it worked differently.) The *shell* is a program that acts as a user interface to DOS. Rather than use the command line to enter commands, you can enter commands through the shell. The shell looks like this:

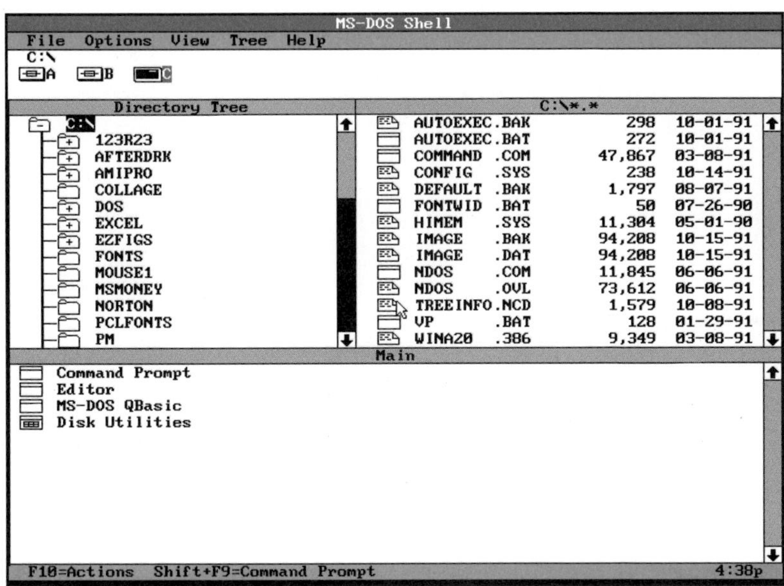

The shell is less intimidating and easier to use than the command prompt. The shell is covered in the last section of the Task/Review part.

Typing a Command

Learning DOS is similar to learning a new language. You have to communicate using words that DOS understands. DOS then takes these words or commands and translates them into a language that the physical components of the machine can understand.

The language you use is called *syntax*. Syntax is the proper format of a command. If you don't get the syntax correct, the command will not work. As you work through the exercises in this book, be careful to type the command (and any spaces) as they appear. If the command doesn't work as discussed, try typing the command again.

Case doesn't matter when you type a command. You can type the command in upper- or lowercase letters. DOS reads COPY, copy, and Copy as the same command.

If you make a mistake when typing, you can press Backspace to delete characters before you press Enter.

Taking Care of the Computer

Take care of the hardware (everything you can see and touch) the same way you would care for your TV or VCR. Don't feed it, water it, drop it, or expose it to extreme heat or cold.

Take care of the software the same way you would take care of audio or video cassettes. Don't leave them in extreme heat, don't spill anything on them, don't open the metal shutter, and keep them away from magnets. Keep in mind that all electrical equipment puts out a magnetic field. This means the telephone, the electric pencil sharpener, and even the personal computer itself. Of course, you don't have to keep your phone in a desk drawer—just don't keep floppy disks near the phone.

Finally, always turn off your machine properly. Never shut off your computer while in the middle of a program:

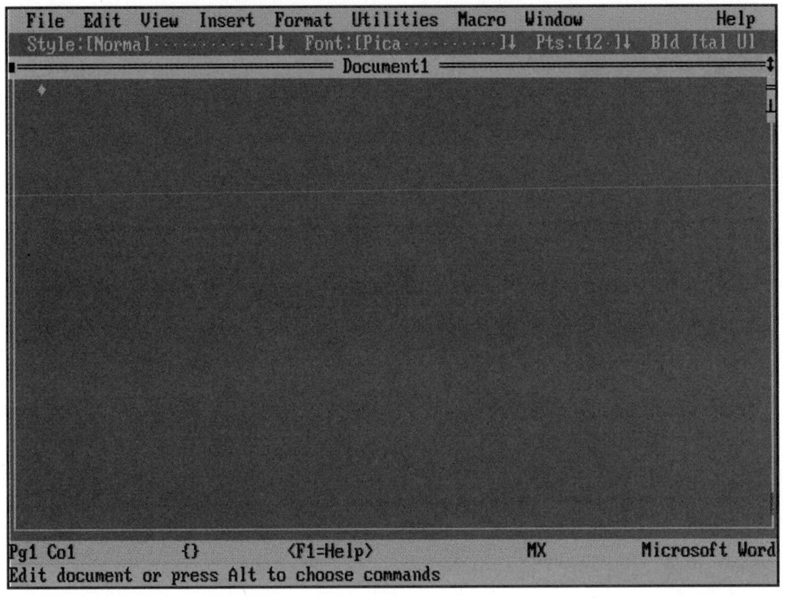

Close any open programs and be sure that you are at the DOS prompt. Then you can turn off your computer:

Task/Review

Learning DOS Basics

Working with Disks

Working with Files

Protecting Your Files

Customizing and Optimizing Your Computer

Using the DOS Shell

Alphabetical Listing of Tasks

Command Tasks

DOS Shell Tasks

Learning DOS Basics

This section includes the following tasks:

Start DOS

Restart DOS

Turn off the computer

Set the prompt to display the current directory

Get help

Display additional help information

Search for a help topic

Exit Help

Display files

Clear the screen

Display a wide file listing

Make a directory

Change directories

Change to the root directory

Display the directory tree

Remove a directory

Pause a file listing

Display selected files

Display directories only

TASK

Start DOS

before

Oops!

If you don't see the DOS prompt, be sure that you turned on both the computer and monitor. If you have plugged the computer and monitor into a power strip, be sure that the strip is plugged in and is turned on.

1. **Turn on the computer and monitor.**

   Every computer has a different location for its On/Off switch. Check the side, the front, and the back of your computer. Your monitor may have a separate On/Off switch; if so, you must turn this switch to On.

   DOS starts automatically when you turn on your computer. You might see information on-screen as DOS goes through its startup routine. Some systems check the memory. You might see something like `256 OK`, `512 OK`, and so on. You might see different commands on-screen.

   DOS starts and then looks for a CONFIG.SYS file. If DOS finds this file, it executes the commands in that file. Then DOS looks for an AUTOEXEC.BAT file. If it finds this file, it executes the commands in that file. (These files are discussed in the Basics part.)

   On some systems, you simply have to turn on the computer. Other systems, however, prompt you for the date and time. In this case, follow steps 2 and 3.

2. **If you are prompted for the date, type the current date and press Enter.**

   When you first turn on the computer, some systems ask you to enter the current date.

after

3. If you are prompted for the time, type the current time and press **Enter**.

   If you are prompted for the date, you will also be prompted for the time.

   You see the DOS prompt on-screen (`C:\>`). The DOS prompt may appear differently on your computer. (You can change the prompt if you want. See *TASK: Set the prompt to display the current directory*.)

Non-System disk error?

If you see the error message `Non-System disk or disk error. Replace and press any key when ready,` you probably have a floppy disk in drive A. Eject this disk and press any key. If this doesn't work, you may have a problem with your disk. See *Using MS-DOS 6*, Special Edition, for more information.

Enter correct date and time

Your computer uses the date and time to keep track of when you save files to disk. Therefore, if the date and time information isn't entered automatically, be sure to enter the correct date and time so that your file information is accurate.

REVIEW

To start DOS

1. Turn on the computer and monitor.
2. If you are prompted, type the current date and press **Enter**.
3. If you are prompted, type the current time and press **Enter**.

TASK

Restart DOS

before

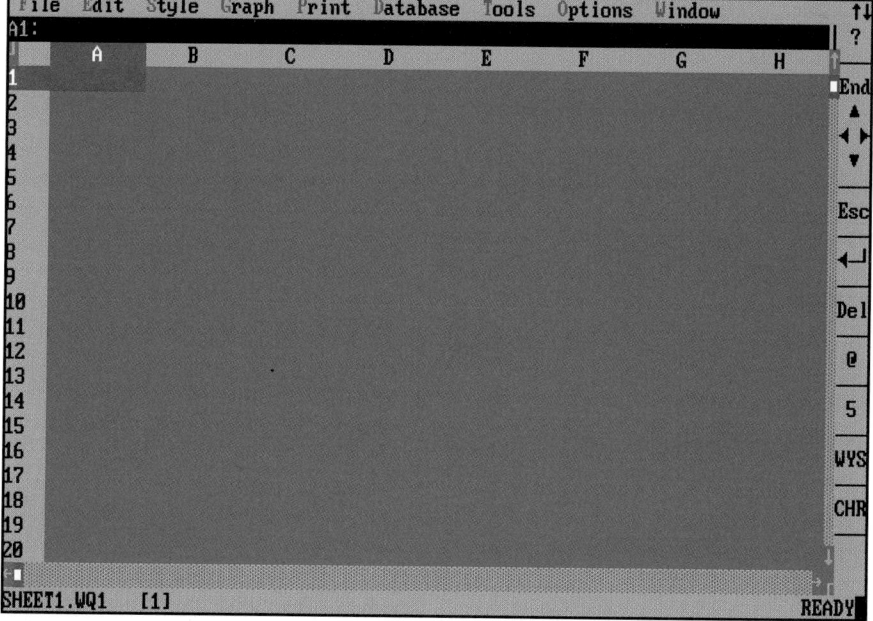

Oops!

If nothing happens when you press these keys, turn off the machine, and then turn it on again.

1. **Press and hold down Ctrl, Alt, and Del.**

   You must press all three keys at once. That is, press and hold down the Ctrl key. Keeping Ctrl held down, press and hold down the Alt key. Then keeping Ctrl and Alt held down, press the Del key. Pressing these three keys together tells DOS to start over.

   (The Before screen shows a spreadsheet application that "froze" and wouldn't respond to commands.)

2. **Release all three keys.**

   This process is called a "warm boot" or a "soft boot." DOS runs through its startup routine and executes the AUTOEXEC.BAT file and CONFIG.SYS. In a warm boot, DOS skips some of the checks it performs during a "cold boot." (A *cold boot* is when you turn off and then on the machine.) A cold boot is harder on your computer. Always try a warm boot first.

   Some computers also have a Reset button. You can press this button to restart the computer.

after

Why restart the computer?

If the system "hangs" (doesn't respond to your commands), you may need to restart. Also, if you change a key file (AUTOEXEC.BAT or CONFIG.SYS), you must reboot to make the changes take effect.

REVIEW

To restart DOS

Press **Ctrl-Alt-Del**.

Be careful!

Using Ctrl-Alt-Del is an escape from some situations, but you should reboot only when nothing else works or only when a program tells you to do so.

TASK

Turn off the computer

before

Oops!

To turn on the computer, see *TASK: Start DOS.*

1. **Exit all programs.**

   You should turn off the computer only when you are at a DOS prompt. If you are working in a program, save all files and exit the program before you turn off the computer. (See your program manual for help with saving and exiting.)

2. **Turn off the computer and the monitor (if necessary).**

   Every computer has a different location for its On/Off switch. Check the side, the front, and the back of your computer. Your monitor may have a separate On/Off switch. If so, you also need to turn this switch to Off.

Should you leave the computer on?

One-half of the computer world says you should leave the computer on most of the time. The other half says you should turn it off each time you finish using it. Each practice has its own benefits. See *Using MS-DOS 6*, Special Edition, for more information.

REVIEW

To turn off the computer

1. Exit all programs so that you return to the DOS prompt.
2. Turn off the computer and monitor.

TASK

before

Set the prompt to display the current directory

Oops!

Type **PROMPT**, and then press Enter to see just the C> prompt.

1. Type **PROMPT**.

   PROMPT is the command that tells DOS what to display when it is ready for a command. The default prompt is C>. If you or someone else has changed your PROMPT command, your prompt might look different.

2. Press the **space bar once**.

   Pressing the space bar once inserts a space between the command and the prompt you want to use.

3. Type **PG**.

   PG is a code that tells DOS to display the current directory. When you change directories, the name of the current directory appears.

   Suppose, for example, that you change to the DATA directory. The prompt will read C:\DATA>. This prompt reminds you where you are within DOS.

4. Press **Enter**.

   Pressing Enter confirms the new prompt. You still see C:\> at the root level, but when you move to a different directory, you see that directory name.

after

Enter a different prompt

You can type anything for the prompt (step 3)—for instance, you can type a greeting (Hi Mike!), a reminder, or any text you want.

REVIEW

To set the prompt to display the current directory

1. Type **PROMPT**.
2. Press the **space bar once**.
3. Type **PG**.
4. Press **Enter**.

Add to AUTOEXEC.BAT

You should add a prompt statement to your AUTOEXEC.BAT file so that you don't have to set the prompt each time you start DOS. See *Using MS-DOS 6,* Special Edition, for more information.

TASK

Get help

before

Oops!

To exit help, see *TASK: Exit Help.*

1. Type **HELP**.

   This is the command to access the Help topics.

2. Press **Enter**.

   This step executes the command. You see a list of DOS commands on-screen. The menu options (File and Search) along the top of the screen enable you to access Help commands.

3. Press the ↓ key until you highlight Copy.

   This step selects the command for which you want help.

4. Press **Enter**.

   This step displays a description of the command and the proper syntax of the command. *Syntax* is the format in which you must type the command. If you use incorrect syntax, the command will not execute.

   As a shortcut, you can also type HELP and then type the name of the command you want. If you type **HELP COPY** and press Enter, for example, DOS will display help on the copy command.

after

```
 File  Search                                                    Help
                          MS-DOS Help: COPY
◄Notes►  ◄Examples►
─────────────────────────────────────────────────────────────────────

                               COPY

Copies one or more files to another location.

This command can also be used to combine files. When more than one file is
copied, MS-DOS displays each filename as the file is copied.

Syntax

    COPY [/A|/B] source [/A|/B] [+ source [/A|/B] [+ ...]][destination
    [/A|/B]] [/V]

Parameters

source
    Specifies the location and name of a file or set of files from which you
    want to copy. Source can consist of a drive letter and colon, a
    directory name, a filename, or a combination.

<Alt+C=Contents> <Alt+N=Next> <Alt+B=Back>                   C  00001:002
```

Display other information

To display other information (Notes and Examples), see *TASK: Move among help information.*

REVIEW

To get help

1. Type **HELP**.
2. Press **Enter**.
3. Use the arrow keys to highlight the topic you want.
4. Press **Enter**.

Version 6 only

This help system is available only with Version 6 of DOS.

Display additional help information

before

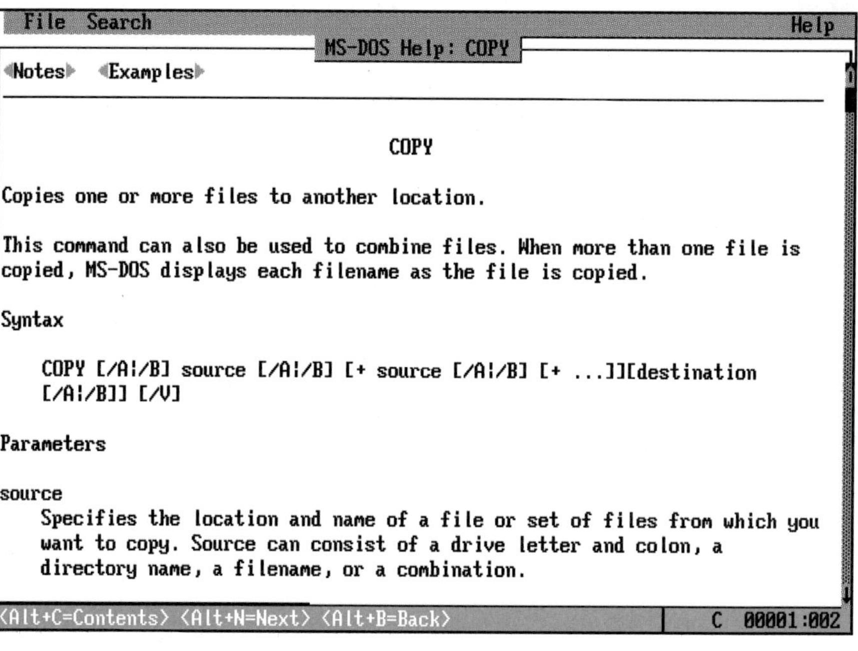

Oops!

To return to the previous topic, press the Alt-B key combination. To display the next topic, press Alt-N. To return to the contents screen, press Alt-C.

1. Display help on the Copy command.

   For information on this step, see *TASK: Get help*. By default, DOS displays the Syntax of the command. You also can display Notes and Examples.

   Syntax displays the format of the command. Notes explains any additional information about the command. Examples shows you some example commands.

   The first option, Notes, is selected. To select a different option, press Tab.

2. Press **Enter**.

   This step selects the Notes option. You see a screen with additional information.

after

```
 File  Search                                                   Help
                      MS-DOS Help: COPY--Notes
◄Examples►  ◄Syntax►
──────────────────────────────────────────────────────────────────

                             COPY—Notes

Copying to and from devices

You can substitute a device name for one or more occurrences of source or
for destination.

Using or omitting the /B switch when copying to a device

When destination is a device (for example, COM1 or LPT1), the /B switch
causes MS-DOS to copy data to the device in binary mode. In binary mode, all
characters (including such special characters as CTRL+C, CTRL+S, CTRL+Z, and
carriage return) are copied to the device as data. Whereas, omission of the
/B switch causes MS-DOS to copy data to the device in ASCII mode. In ASCII
mode, such special characters as those previously listed may cause MS-DOS to
take special action during the copying process.

Using the default destination file
<Alt+C=Contents> <Alt+N=Next> <Alt+B=Back>                 C  00001:002
```

Exit help

See *TASK: Exit Help* for information on exiting help.

REVIEW

To display additional help information

1. Display help on the command you want.
2. Press **Tab** to select the other option (Notes, Examples, or Syntax).
3. Press **Enter**.

Version 6 only

This help system is available only with Version 6 of DOS.

Search for a help topic

before

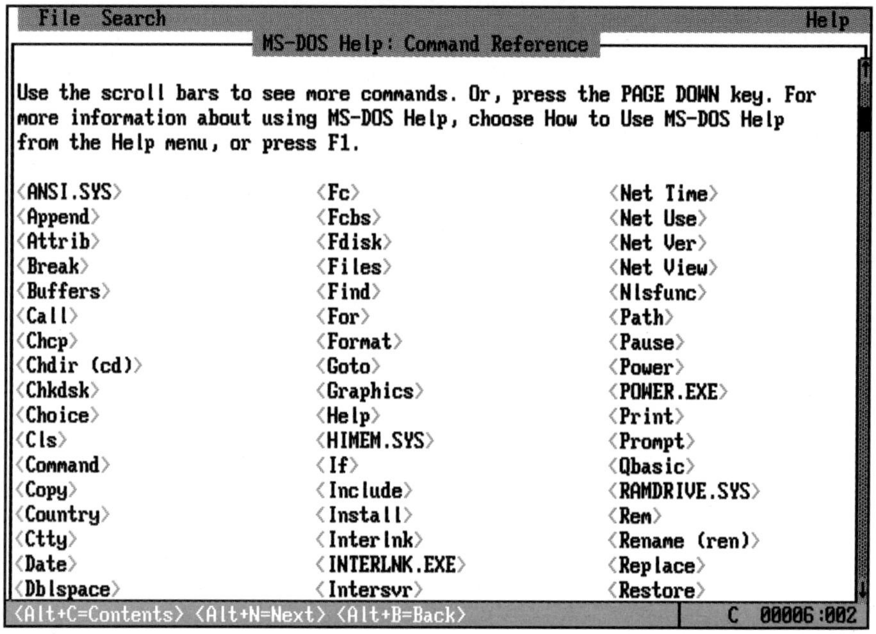

```
 File  Search                                                          Help
                      MS-DOS Help: Command Reference

Use the scroll bars to see more commands. Or, press the PAGE DOWN key. For
more information about using MS-DOS Help, choose How to Use MS-DOS Help
from the Help menu, or press F1.

<ANSI.SYS>                 <Fc>                        <Net Time>
<Append>                   <Fcbs>                      <Net Use>
<Attrib>                   <Fdisk>                     <Net Ver>
<Break>                    <Files>                     <Net View>
<Buffers>                  <Find>                      <Nlsfunc>
<Call>                     <For>                       <Path>
<Chcp>                     <Format>                    <Pause>
<Chdir (cd)>               <Goto>                      <Power>
<Chkdsk>                   <Graphics>                  <POWER.EXE>
<Choice>                   <Help>                      <Print>
<Cls>                      <HIMEM.SYS>                 <Prompt>
<Command>                  <If>                        <Qbasic>
<Copy>                     <Include>                   <RAMDRIVE.SYS>
<Country>                  <Install>                   <Rem>
<Ctty>                     <Interlnk>                  <Rename (ren)>
<Date>                     <INTERLNK.EXE>              <Replace>
<Dblspace>                 <Intersvr>                  <Restore>
<Alt+C=Contents> <Alt+N=Next> <Alt+B=Back>                     C  00006:002
```

Oops!

If DOS cannot find a match, you see the message, `Match not found`. Press Enter, check your typing, and try again.

1. Type **HELP** and press **Enter**.

   This step displays the Help Contents screen.

2. Press **Alt-S**.

   This step opens the Search menu. To press the Alt-S key combination, press and hold down the Alt key. Then type S. Release both keys.

3. Type **F**.

   This step selects the Find command. You see the Find dialog box, and DOS prompts you, `Find What?` Note that you can control how the search is performed.

   To use the other available search options, see *Using MS-DOS 6*, Special Edition.

4. Type **MEM**.

   MEM is the command on which you want help. You also can type the text you want to find. Suppose, for example, that you don't know the name of a specific command but you do know you want information on memory; you can simply type **memory**.

   DOS searches first through the main topics and then scans the other help text to find a match.

after

```
 File  Search                                                        Help
                        MS-DOS Help: MEM
◄Notes►  ◄Examples►
─────────────────────────────────────────────────────────────────────

                              MEM

Displays the amount of used and free memory in your system.

You can use the MEM command to display information about allocated memory
areas, free memory areas, and programs that are currently loaded into
memory.

Syntax

    MEM [/CLASSIFY|/DEBUG|/FREE|/MODULE modulename] [/PAGE]

To display the status of your system's used and free memory, use the
following syntax:

    MEM

Switches
<Alt+C=Contents> <Alt+N=Next> <Alt+B=Back>               C  00001:002
```

5. Press **Enter**.

   This step starts the search. DOS displays information about the command on-screen.

Cancel the search

To cancel the search, press the Esc key.

REVIEW

To search for a help topic

1. Type **HELP** and press **Enter** to start Help.
2. Press **Alt-S** to open the Search menu.
3. Type **F** to select the Find command.
4. Type the command or text you want to find.
5. Press **Enter**.

Exit help

To exit Help, see *TASK: Exit Help*.

Exit Help

before

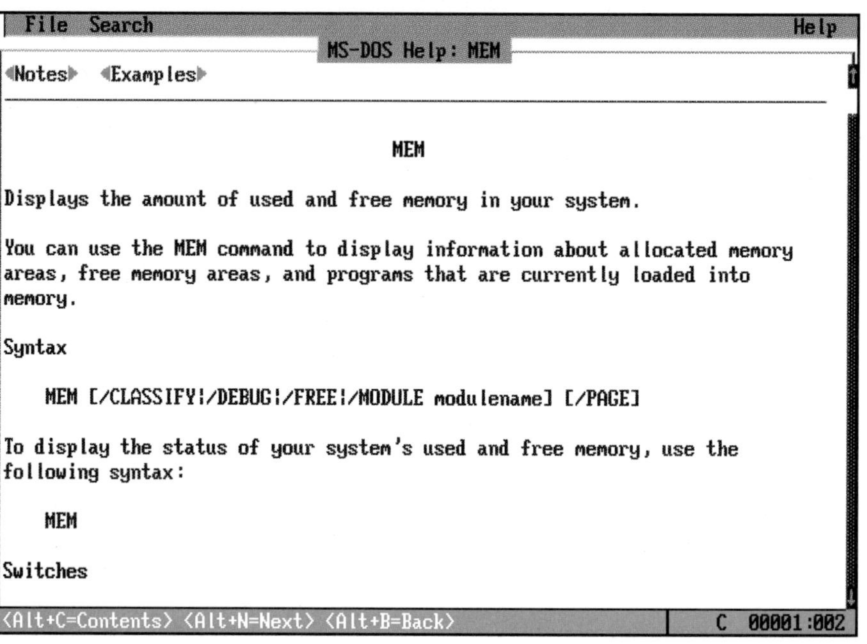
File Search
Help
MS-DOS Help: MEM
◄Notes► ◄Examples►
MEM
Displays the amount of used and free memory in your system.
You can use the MEM command to display information about allocated memory areas, free memory areas, and programs that are currently loaded into memory.
Syntax
MEM [/CLASSIFY¦/DEBUG¦/FREE¦/MODULE modulename] [/PAGE]
To display the status of your system's used and free memory, use the following syntax:
MEM
Switches
<Alt+C=Contents> <Alt+N=Next> <Alt+B=Back>
C 00001:002

1. From any Help screen, press **Alt-F**.

   This step opens the File menu. You see a list of File commands.

2. Type **x**.

   This step selects the Exit command. You exit Help and return to the DOS prompt.

Oops!

To restart help, type **HELP** and press Enter.

after

Get more information

For information on all Help options, see *Using MS-DOS 6,* Special Edition.

REVIEW

To exit Help

1. Press **Alt-F** to open the Help menu.
2. Type **x** to select the Exit command.

Version 6 only

This help system is available only with Version 6 of DOS.

TASK

Display files

before

Oops!

If you see the message `Bad command or file name`, you typed the command incorrectly. Try again.

1. From the DOS prompt, type DIR.

DIR is the directory command. It tells DOS to list all the files in the current directory. In this example, the current directory is the root (or main directory). See *TASK: Change directories* for information on changing the directory.

2. Press Enter.

Pressing Enter confirms the command. You see a list of the files and directories in the root directory. (Your list will vary, depending on the files and directories you have created.)

Notice that the following information appears on-screen:

File name	The root of the file name (up to eight characters) appears first.
Extension	The extension is listed in the second column.
File Size	The next column lists the size of the file. The size is measured in bytes. One byte equals about one character. If the entry is a directory, nothing is listed.
Directory	If the entry is a directory, you see `<DIR>` in the next column.

after

```
C:\>DIR

 Volume in drive C is SEO'S DISK
 Directory of  C:\

HARDCARD     <DIR>      9-04-91  12:10a
DOS          <DIR>      5-18-91  12:16a
CONFIG   SYS        10 10-23-90   1:02a
AUTOEXEC OLD        98  9-04-91  12:49a
DATA         <DIR>      9-04-91  12:39a
COMMAND  COM     25307  3-17-87  12:00p
AUTOEXEC BAT       128  8-28-91  12:02a
TREEINFO NCD       299  9-04-91  12:18a
FRECOVER DAT     38912 10-12-91  12:00a
FRECOVER BAK     38912 10-12-91  12:00a
COLLAGE      <DIR>      8-28-91  12:01a
WORD5        <DIR>      5-18-91  12:03a
NU           <DIR>      5-18-91  12:17a
CHOICE       <DIR>      5-18-91  12:20a
WP51         <DIR>      5-18-91  12:23a
QPRO         <DIR>      6-24-91   2:46a
       16 File(s)  4431872 bytes free

C:\>
```

Date	The next column displays the date when the file was created or modified.
Time	The final column displays the time when the file was created or modified.

The two lines at the end of the directory listing display the number of files, bytes taken, and bytes free (disk space remaining).

The DOS prompt appears at the bottom of the listing so that you can type the next command.

Files scroll off the screen?

If files scroll off the screen (you cannot see the entire list), you have too many files to display on one screen. In this case, display a wide listing (see *TASK: Display a wide file listing*) or pause the display (see *TASK: Pause a file listing*).

REVIEW

To display files

1. From the DOS prompt, type **DIR**.
2. Press **Enter**.

TASK

Clear the screen

before

```
C:\>DIR

 Volume in drive C is SEO'S DISK
 Directory of  C:\

HARDCARD     <DIR>      9-04-91  12:10a
DOS          <DIR>      5-18-91  12:16a
CONFIG   SYS       10  10-23-90   1:02a
AUTOEXEC OLD       98   9-04-91  12:49a
DATA         <DIR>      9-04-91  12:39a
COMMAND  COM    25307   3-17-87  12:00p
AUTOEXEC BAT      128   8-28-91  12:02a
TREEINFO NCD      299   9-04-91  12:18a
FRECOVER DAT    38912  10-12-91  12:00a
FRECOVER BAK    38912  10-12-91  12:00a
COLLAGE      <DIR>      8-28-91  12:01a
WORD5        <DIR>      5-18-91  12:03a
NU           <DIR>      5-18-91  12:17a
CHOICE       <DIR>      5-18-91  12:20a
WP51         <DIR>      5-18-91  12:23a
QPRO         <DIR>      6-24-91   2:46a
       16 File(s)  4431872 bytes free

C:\>
```

Oops!

If you see the message `Bad command or file name`, you typed the command incorrectly. Try again.

1. **From the DOS prompt, type CLS.**

   This step tells DOS to clear the screen.

2. **Press Enter.**

   Pressing Enter confirms the command. The current screen information is cleared so that all you see is the DOS prompt at the top of the screen.

after

REVIEW

To clear the screen

1. At the DOS prompt, type CLS.
2. Press Enter.

TASK

Display a wide file listing

before

Oops!

If you see the message `Bad command or file name` or `Invalid switch`, you did not type the command correctly. Try typing the command again, and be sure that you don't insert a space between the slash and the switch.

1. From the DOS prompt, type **DIR**.

   DIR is the directory command. Typing this command tells DOS to display a directory listing.

2. Press the **space bar once**.

   Pressing the space bar once inserts a space between the command name and the switch. A switch is added to a command to modify how the command works.

3. Type **/W**.

   /W is a switch. Switches are preceded by a slash and modify the command (DIR). In this case, the switch tells DOS to display a wide listing (W). The entire command is DIR /W.

4. Press **Enter**.

   Pressing Enter confirms the command. You see a listing across the screen of the directory contents. (Depending on what files and directories you have created, you will see something different.)

after

```
C:\>DIR /W

 Volume in drive C is HARD DISK
 Volume Serial Number is 1724-0637
 Directory of C:\

[HARDCARD]      [DOS]           CONFIG.SYS      [OLD_DOS.1]     WINA20.386
AUTOEXEC.BAT    TREEINFO.NCD    FRECOVER.DAT    FRECOVER.BAK    [COLLAGE]
[WORD5]         [NU]            [CHOICE]        [WP51]          COMMAND.COM
[QPRO]
       16 file(s)     135489 bytes
                     2744320 bytes free

C:\>
```

Note that only the file or directory name is listed in five columns across the screen. The other file information (size, date, and time) does not appear. In DOS 6, directories appear in brackets. Also in DOS 6, the last two lines display the number of files, number of bytes used, and number of bytes free.

REVIEW

To display a wide file listing

1. At the DOS prompt, type **DIR /W**.
2. Press **Enter**.

TASK

Make a directory

before

Oops!

If you see the message `Directory already exists`, a directory with the same name already exists. Simply give the new directory another name.

1. **At the DOS prompt, type MD.**

   MD is the make directory command. Typing this command tells DOS to create a directory.

2. **Press the space bar once.**

   Pressing the space bar once inserts a space between the command name and the directory name.

3. **Type \DATA.**

   DATA is the name of the directory that you want to create. The backslash tells DOS to make this a directory of the root directory. (The backslash represents the root.)

4. **Press Enter.**

   Pressing Enter confirms the command; DOS creates the directory. The entire command is MD\DATA. Keep in mind that the directory you started from is still the current directory. You return to the DOS prompt.

5. **Type DIR and press Enter.**

   This step displays the directory listing on-screen so that you can see the new directory entry.

after

```
 Volume in drive C is HARD DISK
 Volume Serial Number is 1724-0637
 Directory of C:\

HARDCARD     <DIR>     09-04-91  12:10a
DOS          <DIR>     05-18-91  12:16a
CONFIG   SYS        74 09-04-91  12:49a
DATA         <DIR>     09-04-91  12:24a
OLD_DOS  1   <DIR>     09-04-91  12:39a
WINA20   386      9349 04-09-91   5:00a
AUTOEXEC BAT        98 09-04-91  12:49a
TREEINFO NCD       299 09-04-91  12:18a
FRECOVER DAT     38912 09-04-91  12:00a
FRECOVER BAK     38912 09-04-91  12:00a
COLLAGE      <DIR>     08-28-91  12:01a
WORD5        <DIR>     05-18-91  12:03a
NU           <DIR>     05-18-91  12:17a
CHOICE       <DIR>     05-18-91  12:20a
WP51         <DIR>     05-18-91  12:23a
COMMAND  COM     47845 04-09-91   5:00a
QPRO         <DIR>     06-24-91   2:46a
       17 file(s)     135489 bytes
                     2711552 bytes free

C:\>
```

Where are new directories created?

The directory is created within the current directory if you don't type the entire path. For instance, if you forget the backslash, the directory is placed in the current directory—which may not be the root directory.

REVIEW

To make a directory

1. At the DOS prompt, type **MD**.
2. Press the **space bar once**.
3. Type the complete name of the directory (including the backslash and the path).
4. Press **Enter**.

Change directories

To change directories, see *TASK: Change directories.*

TASK

Change directories

before

Oops!

If you see the message `Invalid directory`, you may have typed the command incorrectly or typed a directory that does not exist. Try typing the command again.

1. At the DOS prompt, type **CD**.

   CD is the change directory command. Typing this command tells DOS to change to a different directory.

2. Press the **space bar once**.

   Pressing the space bar once inserts a space between the command name and the directory name.

3. Type **\DATA**.

   \DATA is the directory name. If you don't have a directory with this name, type the name of a directory that you do have. (To create the DATA directory, see *TASK: Make a directory*.)

4. Press **Enter**.

   Pressing Enter confirms the command. The entire command is CD\DATA.

   If your prompt displays the current directory, you see `C:\DATA>`. This prompt reminds you that you are in the DATA directory. (Your prompt may display only `C:\>`. To make your prompt display the current directory name, see *TASK: Set the prompt to display the current directory*.)

after

Type the entire path

The path tells DOS where to find the directory, so you must type the entire path or route to the command. If the directory is part of another directory, you must type the entire name. For example, if DATA is contained in the directory WORD, you must type

After you are in the new directory, you can display a directory listing, start a program, or copy files. CD is an important command. This command enables you to navigate around the directory structure by moving from directory to directory.

REVIEW

To change directories

1. At the DOS prompt, type **CD**.
2. Press the **space bar once**.
3. Type the directory name. Be sure to type the entire path.
4. Press **Enter**.

Try this tip...

To back up one directory (move to the directory that contains the current directory), type CD.. (two periods). This command tells DOS to move back one directory. For instance, if you are at the C:\WP\DATA> prompt, typing CD.. takes you to the C:\WP> prompt (directory).

TASK

Change to the root directory

before

Oops!

If you see the message `Bad command or file name`, you might not have typed the command correctly. Try typing the command again.

1. At the DOS prompt, type **CD**.

   CD is the change directory command. Typing this command tells DOS to make a different directory active.

2. Type ****.

   The backslash (\) is the name for the root directory. Typing this command tells DOS that you want to return to the root directory.

3. Press **Enter**.

   Pressing Enter confirms the command. You return to the root directory.

after

Return from any directory

You can return to the root directory from any other directory by typing this command.

REVIEW

To change to the root directory

1. From the DOS prompt, type CD\.
2. Press Enter.

Invalid switch?

If you see the message `Invalid Switch`, you typed a forward slash (/) instead of a backward slash (\).

TASK

Display the directory tree

before

Oops!

If you see the message `Bad command or file name`, you typed the command incorrectly. Try typing the command again.

1. Type **CD**.

   This step starts you at the root directory on drive C. See *TASK: Change to the root directory* if you need help with this step.

2. Type **TREE**.

   TREE is the tree directory command. Typing this command tells DOS to display only the directory names in a tree format. A tree format shows which directories contain other directories.

3. Press **Enter**.

   Pressing Enter confirms the command. You see a map of your directory structure. Each directory name is listed. Directories within directories are also displayed; lines show how the directories are organized.

after

```
C:\>TREE
Directory PATH listing for Volume HARD DISK
Volume Serial Number is 1724-0637
C:.
├───HARDCARD
├───DOS
├───DATA
├───OLD_DOS.1
├───COLLAGE
│   └───FIGURES
├───WORD5
│   └───WORK
├───NU
├───CHOICE
├───WP51
│   ├───MACROS
│   ├───GRAPHICS
│   ├───MISC
│   ├───BOOK
│   └───CLASS
└───QPRO
    └───HOUSE

C:\>
```

Display subdirectory trees

If you are in a directory other than the root, typing **TREE** lists the subdirectories in that directory (if any exist).

REVIEW

To display the directory tree

1. Type **TREE**.
2. Press **Enter**.

TASK

Remove a directory

before

Oops!

You cannot delete the current directory. (It is similar to trying to saw off a branch that you are standing on!) You must type the command from the root directory or another directory.

1. Type **RD**.

   RD is the remove directory command. Typing this command tells DOS to remove an empty directory.

2. Press the **space bar once**.

   Pressing the space bar once inserts a space between the command name and the directory name.

3. Type **\DATA**.

   DATA is the name of the directory that you want to remove. The entire command is RD \DATA. If you do not have a directory named DATA, type the name of a directory that you do have. Make sure that it is a directory you no longer need. (To create the DATA directory, see *TASK: Make a directory*.)

4. Press **Enter**.

   Pressing Enter confirms the command. The directory is removed.

5. Type **DIR** and press **Enter**.

   This step displays a directory listing so that you can verify that the directory is removed.

after

```
Volume in drive C is HARD DISK
Volume Serial Number is 1724-0637
Directory of C:\

HARDCARD      <DIR>      09-04-91  12:10a
DOS           <DIR>      05-18-91  12:16a
CONFIG   SYS          74 09-04-91  12:49a
OLD_DOS  1    <DIR>      09-04-91  12:39a
WINA20   386        9349 04-09-91   5:00a
AUTOEXEC BAT          98 09-04-91  12:49a
TREEINFO NCD         299 09-04-91  12:18a
FRECOVER DAT       38912 09-04-91  12:00a
FRECOVER BAK       38912 09-04-91  12:00a
COLLAGE       <DIR>      08-28-91  12:01a
WORD5         <DIR>      05-18-91  12:03a
NU            <DIR>      05-18-91  12:17a
CHOICE        <DIR>      05-18-91  12:20a
WP51          <DIR>      05-18-91  12:23a
COMMAND  COM       47845 04-09-91   5:00a
QPRO          <DIR>      06-24-91   2:46a
       16 file(s)     135489 bytes
                     2621440 bytes free

C:\>
```

Delete all files

Before you remove a directory, you must delete all files in that directory. The directory in this example (DATA) didn't contain any files. If it did, you would see an error message. In this case, delete all files. (See *TASK: Delete all files*.) Then try this task again.

REVIEW

To remove a directory

1. Type **RD** and the directory name.
2. Press the **space bar once**.
3. Press **Enter**.

Remove subdirectories

If you have trouble removing a directory, that directory might contain other directories. When you type **DEL *.***, you delete all the files, but you don't remove the directories. You must use the RD (remove directory) command to remove the directories.

TASK

Pause a file listing

before

Oops!

If the directory listing is only one screen, you do not see the message `Press any key to continue`. In this case, you don't need to pause the display.

1. **Type CD \DOS.**

   This command tells DOS to change to the directory named DOS. You should have a directory that contains your DOS file. This directory might be named something different (such as BIN). If so, type that name rather than DOS.

2. **Press Enter.**

   Pressing Enter changes the current directory to DOS. This directory contains several files. You see the prompt `C:\DOS>`.

3. **Type DIR /P.**

   DIR is the directory command and /P is a switch. Switches are preceded by a slash and modify the command (DIR). In this case, the switch tells DOS to display one screen of information and then pause.

4. **Press Enter.**

   Pressing Enter confirms the command. You see a list of DOS files. The message at the bottom of the file list tells you how to continue: `Press any key to continue...`

after

```
Volume in drive C is HARD DISK
Volume Serial Number is 1724-0637
Directory of C:\DOS

.            <DIR>     05-18-91  12:16a
..           <DIR>     05-18-91  12:16a
EGA      SYS      4885 04-09-91   5:00a
FORMAT   COM     32911 04-09-91   5:00a
NLSFUNC  EXE      7052 04-09-91   5:00a
COUNTRY  SYS     17069 04-09-91   5:00a
DISPLAY  SYS     15792 04-09-91   5:00a
EGA      CPI     58873 04-09-91   5:00a
BASIC    COM      1063 03-17-87  12:00p
BASICA   COM     36403 03-17-87  12:00p
HIMEM    SYS     11552 04-09-91   5:00a
KEYB     COM     14986 04-09-91   5:00a
KEYBOARD SYS     34697 04-09-91   5:00a
MODE     COM     23537 04-09-91   5:00a
SETVER   EXE     12007 09-04-91  12:49a
ANSI     SYS      9029 04-09-91   5:00a
DEBUG    EXE     20634 04-09-91   5:00a
DOSKEY   COM      5883 04-09-91   5:00a
EDLIN    EXE     12642 04-09-91   5:00a
Press any key to continue . . .
```

5. Press **Enter**.

   Pressing Enter tells DOS to display the next screenful of information. You can press another key instead of Enter—for instance, the space bar.

6. Continue pressing **Enter** until all files have been displayed.

   When all files are listed, you return to the DOS prompt.

REVIEW

To pause a file listing

1. Change to the directory that you want to list.
2. Type **DIR /P**.
3. Press **Enter**.
4. Continue pressing **Enter** until all files are displayed.

TASK

Display selected files

before

Oops!

If you see the message `File not found`, no files matched the file spec you typed. Try the command again or specify other files to find.

1. Type **CD \DOS**.

   This command changes to the DOS directory. The DOS directory contains DOS files. If you don't have a directory named DOS, type the name of a directory that you do have.

2. Press **Enter**.

   Pressing Enter confirms the command. The current directory is now DOS.

3. Type **DIR *.SYS**.

   The DIR command tells DOS to list files. The rest of the command tells DOS which files to list. In this case, the command tells DOS to list files with any file name. (The asterisk is a wild card. It matches any characters and any number of characters.) The files must have the extension SYS. *.SYS is sometimes called a file spec—it specifies which files to include.

4. Press **Enter**.

   Pressing Enter confirms the command. You see only the SYS files in the directory. If the list is longer than a screenful, it will scroll off the screen.

after

```
C:\DOS>DIR *.SYS

 Volume in drive C is HARD DISK
 Volume Serial Number is 1724-0637
 Directory of C:\DOS

EGA      SYS      4885 04-09-91   5:00a
COUNTRY  SYS     17069 04-09-91   5:00a
DISPLAY  SYS     15792 04-09-91   5:00a
HIMEM    SYS     11552 04-09-91   5:00a
KEYBOARD SYS     34697 04-09-91   5:00a
ANSI     SYS      9029 04-09-91   5:00a
RAMDRIVE SYS      5873 04-09-91   5:00a
SMARTDRV SYS      8335 04-09-91   5:00a
VDISK    SYS      3455 03-17-87  12:00p
DRIVER   SYS      5409 04-09-91   5:00a
PRINTER  SYS     18804 04-09-91   5:00a
       11 file(s)     134900 bytes
                     2539520 bytes free

C:\DOS>
```

Too many parameters?

If you see the command, `Too many parameters`, you typed the command in the wrong format. Do not insert spaces between wild cards or the extension.

REVIEW

To display selected files

1. From the DOS prompt, type **DIR** followed by the file or files that you want to display. Use wild cards (* and ?) if you want.
2. Press **Enter**.

Display other files

Use this same procedure to list other files. For example, type **DIR S*.*** to list all files that start with S and have any extension. Type **DIR FO*.COM** to match all files that start with FO and have the extension COM. Type **DIR ASSIGN.COM** to display the file named ASSIGN.COM.

TASK

before

Display directories only

Oops!

If you see the command `Too many parameters`, you typed the command in the wrong format. Retype the command, and be sure not to insert spaces between wild cards or the extension.

1. From the DOS prompt, type **DIR *.** (period).

   This command tells DOS to display a directory (DIR). The rest of the command is the file spec; it tells DOS which files to list. The first part of the command tells DOS to display files with any name. (The asterisk is a wild card and matches any other characters.) The second part of the command tells DOS to list files with no extension (nothing following the period). Be sure to type the period.

2. Press **Enter**.

   Pressing Enter confirms the command. You see a list of all files with any file name and no extension. In most cases, directories don't have extensions, so this command should display the directories on disk. (If this directory contains some files without extensions, these files also will be listed.)

after

```
C:\>DIR *.

 Volume in drive C is HARD DISK
 Volume Serial Number is 1724-0637
 Directory of C:\

HARDCARD     <DIR>      09-04-91  12:10a
DOS          <DIR>      05-18-91  12:16a
COLLAGE      <DIR>      08-28-91  12:01a
WORD5        <DIR>      05-18-91  12:03a
NU           <DIR>      05-18-91  12:17a
CHOICE       <DIR>      05-18-91  12:20a
WP51         <DIR>      05-18-91  12:23a
QPRO         <DIR>      06-24-91   2:46a
        8 file(s)          0 bytes
                     2506752 bytes free

C:\>
```

Display all directories

With DOS 5, and 6, you also can use the command **DIR/A:D** to display all directories.

REVIEW

To display directories only

1. From the DOS prompt, type DIR *. (period).
2. Press Enter.

Forget the period?

If you type just **DIR*** without the period, all files and directories are listed—just as if you typed **DIR**.

Working with Disks

This section covers the following tasks:

Insert a disk

Format a disk

Change drives

Copy a disk

TASK

before

Insert a disk

Oops!

You must shut the disk door. If the door isn't shut, the drive cannot read the disk.

1. Hold the disk so that the label is facing up.

Just as you shouldn't insert a videocassette tape upside down, you also shouldn't insert a floppy disk upside down.

If you are are using a 5 1/4-inch disk that doesn't have a label, hold the disk so that the notched side is on the left. (Disk types are described in the Basics part.)

If you are using a 3 1/2-inch disk that does not have a label, look for writing (disk type, arrow, manufacturer, for instance) to indicate the "up" side. Hold the disk so that you see the writing.

2. Insert the disk into the drive.

Push the disk gently—don't force it. With a 3 1/2-inch disk, you should hear a click, indicating the disk is inserted (skip step 3). For 5 1/4-inch disks, you must follow an additional step (step 3).

3. If necessary, shut the drive door.

The drive door has a lever or latch. Push the lever so that it is closed.

after

4. Type A: and press **Enter**.

This step makes floppy drive A (where you inserted the disk) active. If you inserted the disk into a different floppy disk drive (such as B), type that name instead. DOS displays `A:\>` to tell you that a disk is inserted properly into the drive.

Drive door will not shut?

You cannot shut the lever if a disk is not inserted properly into the drive (5 1/4-inch disks).

REVIEW

To insert a disk

1. Hold the disk label up.
2. Insert the disk into the drive.
3. If necessary, shut the drive door.

TASK

Format a disk

before

Oops!

To cancel the format, press Ctrl-Break for step 6 in the TASK section.

1. **Insert a blank disk into drive A.**

   Be sure that the disk is blank (or contains information that you no longer need). Formatting wipes out all the information on the disk. For help inserting the disk, see *TASK: Insert a disk*.

2. **Type FORMAT.**

   FORMAT is the command that prepares a disk for use.

3. **Press the space bar once.**

   This step inserts a space between the command and the drive to format.

4. **Type A:.**

   Drive A contains the disk that you want to format. Be sure not to format drive C.

5. **Press Enter.**

   Pressing Enter confirms the command. You see the message `Insert new diskette for drive A: and press ENTER when ready.`

6. **Press Enter.**

   Pressing Enter tells DOS that the disk has been inserted. The formatting procedure begins. Depending on your DOS version, different things may happen. When the format is complete, you see the message `Format complete.`

after

```
C:\>FORMAT A:
Insert new diskette for drive A:
and press ENTER when ready...

Checking existing disk format.
Saving UNFORMAT information.
Verifying 720K
Format complete.

Volume label (11 characters, ENTER for none)? DATA DISK

    730112 bytes total disk space
    730112 bytes available on disk

      1024 bytes in each allocation unit.
       713 allocation units available on disk.

Volume Serial Number is 2A34-07E7

Format another (Y/N)?
```

7. If prompted for a volume label, type **DATA DISK** for the volume label and press **Enter**.

   Depending on the version of DOS you are using, you may not be prompted for a volume label. This label simply assigns a name to the disk. You can press Enter to skip adding a name.

   After the volume label is displayed, you see other information (total disk space, allocation units, and so on). Then you see the message `Format another (Y/N)?`

8. Type **N** and press **Enter**.

   This step tells DOS that you are finished formatting. You return to the DOS prompt.

Be careful!

You will not be warned if the disk that you are formatting contains information. Be sure to insert a blank disk or a disk that contains information you no longer need.

Unformat a disk

With DOS 5 and 6, you may be able to unformat a disk. See *Using MS-DOS 6*, Special Edition, for complete information.

REVIEW

To format a disk

1. Insert a blank disk into drive A.
2. Type **FORMAT**.
3. Press the **space bar once**.
4. Type the drive name that contains the disk to format.
5. Press **Enter twice**.
6. If prompted, type a volume label and press **Enter**.
7. Type **N** and press **Enter**.

TASK

Change drives

before

Oops!

If you see the message `Not ready reading drive A Abort, Retry, Fail?`, you might not have inserted the disk, might have inserted it improperly, or might have forgotten to shut the drive door. Insert a disk and type R to retry.

1. Insert a formatted disk into drive A.

You may have just one drive. In this case, it is drive A. If you have more than one drive, drive A is usually the top drive of the computer. See *TASK: Insert a disk*.

A formatted disk is a disk that has been prepared for use. If you need to format a disk, see *TASK: Format a disk*.

2. Type A:.

Typing A: specifies the drive that you want to change to (drive A). The name of a drive consists of two parts: the letter and a colon. Be sure not to insert a space between the two items.

3. Press Enter.

Pressing Enter confirms the command. You see `A:\>` on-screen. This prompt reminds you that drive A is the current drive.

after

Why change drives?

You need to change drives when you want to access files on another drive. For example, you might want to copy the files on the disk in drive A to drive C (or vice versa). You might want to display the files on the disk in drive

REVIEW

To change drives

1. Insert a disk into the drive.
2. Type the drive letter followed by a colon (such as A:, B:, or C:).
3. Press Enter.

Disk isn't formatted?

If the disk hasn't been formatted, you see the message `General failure reading drive A Abort, Retry, Fail?` Remove the unformatted disk, insert a formatted disk, and type **R**.

TASK

Copy a disk

(Part 1 of 2)

before

Oops!

You cannot copy a disk from one floppy drive to another floppy drive unless the disks are the same size (3 1/2- or 5 1/4-inch) and capacity.

Copying a disk is a two-part process. The first part, Enter the command, is covered on these two pages. Turn the page for the second part, Swap disks.

1. Insert a disk into drive A.

   Insert a disk that contains files you want to copy. For help inserting the disk, see *TASK: Insert a disk*.

2. Type **DISKCOPY**.

   The DISKCOPY command tells DOS to copy everything on the disk. This process copies the files, the file storage information, and the tracks—technical information about how the data is stored.

3. Press the **space bar once**.

   Pressing the space bar once inserts a space between the command and the drive.

4. Type **A:**.

   Drive A contains the disk that you want to copy.

after

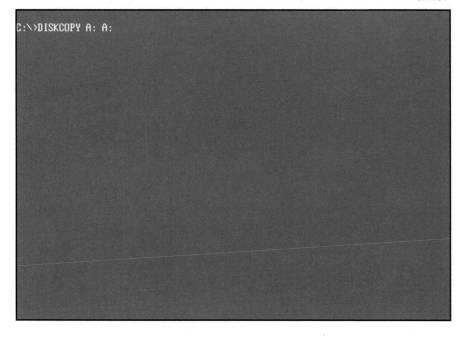

5. **Press the space bar once.**

   Pressing the space bar inserts a space between the source disk (the disk you are copying) and the target disk (the disk you are copying to).

6. **Type A:.**

   Drive A will also contain the disk to which you want to copy. You will swap disks back and forth.

REVIEW

To copy a disk

(Part 1 of 2)

1. Insert the disk you want to copy into drive A.
2. Type **DISKCOPY A:**.
3. Press the **space bar once**.
4. Type **A:**.

Copy a disk

(Part 2 of 2)

before

Oops!

To cancel the copy procedure, press Ctrl-Break at step 2 of the TASK section.

Copying a disk is a two-part process. The first part, Enter the command, is covered on the preceding two pages. These pages cover the second part, Swap Disks.

1. **Press Enter.**

   Pressing Enter confirms the command. You see the message `Insert SOURCE diskette in drive A: Press any key to continue.`

2. **Press Enter.**

   Pressing Enter confirms that you have inserted the source disk. (You inserted the source disk in step 1.)

   You see information about the copy in progress. (For definitions of tracks and sectors, see *Using MS-DOS 6*, Special Edition.) DOS copies part of the disk and then prompts you to insert the target disk with the message `Insert TARGET diskette in drive A: Press any key to continue.`

3. **Eject the disk, insert the target disk, and press Enter.**

   You eject a 3 1/2-inch disk by pressing the button near the disk slot. You eject a 5 1/2-inch disk by opening the drive door.

   The target disk is the disk on which you want the copy placed.

after

```
Insert SOURCE diskette in drive A:

Press any key to continue . . .

Copying 80 tracks
9 sectors per track, 2 side(s)

Insert TARGET diskette in drive A:

Press any key to continue . . .

Insert SOURCE diskette in drive A:

Press any key to continue . . .

Insert TARGET diskette in drive A:

Press any key to continue . . .

Volume Serial Number is 07E9-1C5B

Copy another diskette (Y/N)? N

C:\>
```

4. Continue ejecting and inserting the appropriate disk as prompted.

   Depending on how many bytes the disk holds and the amount of memory on your computer, you may have to swap disks several times. When the disk has been completely copied, you may see a volume serial number. You also see the message `Copy another diskette (Y/N)?`

5. Type **N**.

   Typing N tells DOS that you do not want to copy another disk.

Copy software

When you purchase new software, use this command to make copies of the disks; then use only the copies. This method protects your original disks.

REVIEW

To copy a disk

(Part 2 of 2)

1. Press **Enter** to confirm the command.
2. Press **Enter** to start the copy.
3. Eject the source disk and insert the target disk when prompted.
4. Continue swapping disks until the disk is copied.
5. Type **N** when prompted `Copy another diskette (Y/N)?` if you do not want to copy another disk. Type **Y** if you want to copy another disk.

Working with Files

This section contains the following tasks:

Display file contents

Copy a file

Copy a file to another directory

Copy a group of files to another directory

Copy all files to a different drive

Rename a file

Delete a file

Delete all files

Undelete a file

TASK

Display file contents

before

1. Type **CD** and press **Enter**.

   This step changes to the root directory. For help with this step, see *TASK: Change to the root directory*.

2. Type **TYPE**.

   The TYPE command tells DOS to display the contents of a file.

3. Press the **space bar once**.

   Pressing the space bar once inserts a space between the command and the file that you want to display.

4. Type **AUTOEXEC.BAT**.

   AUTOEXEC.BAT is the name of the file you want to display.

5. Press **Enter**.

   Pressing Enter confirms the command. You see on-screen the contents of the file named AUTOEXEC.BAT. (You may have different commands in your AUTOEXEC.BAT file.)

   The TYPE command only displays the contents of a file. You cannot edit the file.

Oops!

If the file scrolls off the screen, stop the file display by pressing the Ctrl-S key combination. Restart by pressing Ctrl-S again.

after

```
C:\>CD\

C:\>TYPE AUTOEXEC.BAT
ECHO OFF
PROMPT $P$G
date
time
PATH C:\DOS;C:\;C:\NU;c:\WORD5;C:\WP51;c:\collage
FR /SAVE


C:\>
```

Do you hear beeps?

Some files (especially program files) contain characters that DOS cannot display. You may hear beeps and see strange characters on-screen if you display this type of file. Press Ctrl-C to stop the display.

REVIEW

To display file contents

1. Change to the directory that contains the file you want to display.
2. Type **TYPE**, followed by the complete file name (file name and extension) you want to display.
3. Press **Enter**.

File not found?

If you see the message `File not found`, you probably typed the file name incorrectly. Try again. Be sure to type the complete file name, including the extension.

Copy a file

before

C:\>COPY AUTOEXEC.BAT AUTOEXEC.OLD

Oops!

If you see the message `File cannot be copied onto itself`, you either left off the name for the new file or typed the same name for the new file as the original file. You must type the current file name and the name of the copy. Try the command again.

1. Type **CD** and press **Enter**.

   This step changes to the root directory. For help with this step, see *TASK: Change to the root directory*.

2. Type **COPY**.

   The COPY command tells DOS to make a copy of the file.

3. Press the **space bar once**.

   Pressing the space bar once inserts a space between the command name and the next part of the command (the file name).

4. Type **AUTOEXEC.BAT**.

   AUTOEXEC.BAT is the name of the file you want to copy.

5. Press the **space bar once**.

   Pressing the space bar once inserts a space between the file name and the next part of the command (the file name for the new file).

6. Type **AUTOEXEC.OLD**.

   AUTOEXEC.OLD is the name you want to assign the copy of the file. The total command is COPY AUTOEXEC.BAT AUTOEXEC.OLD. This command makes a copy of the file AUTOEXEC.BAT and names the file AUTOEXEC.OLD.

after

```
C:\>COPY AUTOEXEC.BAT AUTOEXEC.OLD
        1 file(s) copied

C:\>DIR AUTOEXEC.*

 Volume in drive C is HARD DISK
 Volume Serial Number is 1724-0637
 Directory of C:\

AUTOEXEC OLD        98 09-04-91  12:49a
AUTOEXEC BAT        98 09-04-91  12:49a
        2 file(s)        196 bytes
                     2367488 bytes free

C:\>
```

7. Press **Enter**.

   Pressing Enter confirms the command. You see the message `1 file(s) copied`. Now you have two versions of the same file. Each has a different name. To confirm that a copy has been made, follow the next step.

8. Type **DIR AUTOEXEC.*** and press **Enter**.

   This command tells DOS to display all files with the file name AUTOEXEC and with any extension. You should see both AUTOEXEC.BAT and AUTOEXEC.OLD.

Copy a file to another directory

To copy a file to another directory, see *TASK: Copy a file to another directory*.

REVIEW

To copy a file

1. Change to the directory that contains the file.
2. Type **COPY**.
3. Press the **space bar once**.
4. Type the name of the file you want to copy.
5. Press the **space bar once**.
6. Type the name of the file for the copy. If necessary, first type the path, the drive letter, or both.
7. Press **Enter**.

TASK

Copy a file to another directory

before

C:\>CD\
C:\>COPY AUTOEXEC.OLD C:\DATA

1. Type **CD** and press **Enter**.

   This step changes to the root directory. For help with this step, see *TASK: Change to the root directory*.

2. Type **COPY**.

   The COPY command tells DOS to make a copy of the file.

3. Press the **space bar once**.

   Pressing the space bar once inserts a space between the command name and the next part of the command.

4. Type **AUTOEXEC.OLD**.

   AUTOEXEC.OLD is the name of the file you want to copy. If you don't have a file by this name, type the name of a file that you do have.

5. Press the **space bar once**.

   Pressing the space bar once inserts a space between the file name and the next part of the command (the directory for the new file).

6. Type **C:\DATA**.

   Typing C:\DATA tells DOS to place the copy in the directory C:\DATA. The file will have the same name.

Oops!

If you see the message `File not found`, the file name could not be found. Be sure you are in the correct directory (the directory that contains the file). Then try the command again.

after

```
C:\>CD\

C:\>COPY AUTOEXEC.OLD C:\DATA
        1 file(s) copied

C:\>CD\DATA

C:\DATA>DIR

 Volume in drive C is HARD DISK
 Volume Serial Number is 1724-0637
 Directory of C:\DATA

.            <DIR>      09-04-91  12:39a
..           <DIR>      09-04-91  12:39a
AUTOEXEC OLD         98 09-04-91  12:49a
        3 file(s)          98 bytes
                     2326528 bytes free

C:\DATA>
```

7. Press **Enter**.

   Pressing Enter confirms the command. You see the message `1 file(s) copied`. Now you have two versions of the same file: one in the root directory and one in the DATA directory. Both files have the same name. (Note in the After screen that the DIR command was used so that you can see the two copies of the file.)

Give the file a different name

You can name the file something different by typing the new file name after the path (step 6 in the TASK section).

REVIEW

To copy a file to another directory

1. Change to the directory that contains the file you want to copy.
2. Type **COPY**.
3. Press the **space bar once**.
4. Type the name of the file you want to copy.
5. Press the **space bar once**.
6. Type the path—the directory where you want to store the copy. If you want to name the file something different from the original name, type the path and the new file name.
7. Press **Enter**.

TASK

Copy a group of files to another directory

before

Oops!

If you see the message `Bad command or file name`, you might have typed the command incorrectly. Try typing the command again, and be sure to insert spaces between the command, the original file name, and the file name for the copy.

1. **From the root directory, type COPY.**

   The COPY command tells DOS to make a copy of the file.

2. **Press the space bar once.**

   Pressing the space bar once inserts a space between the command name and the next part of the command (the file name).

3. **Type *.BAT.**

   After the COPY command, you type the name of the file you want to copy. In this case, you tell DOS to copy a group of files. The files can have any file name, but they must have the extension BAT.

4. **Press the space bar once.**

   Pressing the space bar once inserts a space between the file name and the next part of the command (the path for the new files).

5. **Type C:\DATA.**

   C:\DATA is the path name. This command tells DOS to copy all files with a BAT extension to the directory DATA. (You may have just one file with this extension.) The files will have the same name.

after

```
C:\>COPY *.BAT C:\DATA
AUTOEXEC.BAT
Q.BAT
WS4.BAT
        3 file(s) copied

C:\>
```

6. Press **Enter**.

   Pressing Enter confirms the command. Now you have two versions of each BAT file: one in the original directory and one in the new directory (DATA).

Copy files to a different drive

Use these same steps to copy a group of files to another drive. To do so, type the new drive name for step 5 in the Task section (for example, **A:**). You don't have to type the file name. If you leave off the file name, DOS uses the same namefor the files.

Type the directory correctly

Be sure to type a directory name. If the directory does not exist or is typed incorrectly, DOS adds all the files together and places them in another file. If you type **DAT**, for example, all files would be placed in a file (not directory) named DAT.

REVIEW

To copy a group of files to another directory

1. Type **COPY**.
2. Press the **space bar once**.
3. Type the name of the files you want to copy. Use the asterisk wild card (*) to match any characters. Use the question mark wild card (?) to match a single character.
4. Press the **space bar once**.
5. Type the name of the directory in which you want to place the files.
6. Press **Enter**.

TASK

Copy all files to a different drive

before

Oops!

If you see the message `Not ready drive A,` be sure that you inserted a formatted disk into drive A. Type **R** to retry the command.

1. **Insert a formatted disk into drive A.**

   For help with this step, see *TASK: Insert a disk*.

2. **Type CD\DATA.**

   Typing this command tells DOS to switch to the DATA directory.

3. **Press Enter.**

   Pressing Enter confirms the command. The current directory is now DATA.

4. **Type COPY.**

   COPY is the copy command. It tells DOS to copy files.

5. **Press the space bar once.**

   Pressing the space bar once inserts a space between the command name and the next part of the command (the files to copy).

6. **Type *.*.**

   After the COPY command, you type the name of the file you want to copy. In this case, you tell DOS to copy all files (*.* matches all files).

7. **Press the space bar once.**

   The space bar inserts a space between the file name and the next part of the command (the destination for the files).

after

```
C:\>CD\DATA

C:\DATA>COPY *.* A:
AUTOEXEC.OLD
AUTOEXEC.BAT
Q.BAT
WS4.BAT
        4 file(s) copied

C:\DATA>A:

A:\>DIR

 Volume in drive A is DATA DISK
 Volume Serial Number is 07E9-1C5B
 Directory of A:\

AUTOEXEC OLD        98 09-04-91  12:49a
AUTOEXEC BAT        98 09-04-91  12:49a
Q        BAT       128 08-28-91  12:01a
WS4      BAT       128 08-28-91  12:02a
        4 file(s)         452 bytes
                       726016 bytes free

A:\>
```

8. Type **A:**.

   A: is the drive name for drive A. This command tells DOS to copy all files to drive A. The files will have the same name.

9. Press **Enter**.

   Pressing Enter confirms the command. Now you have two versions of each file: one in the original directory (DATA) and one on drive A.

10. Type **A:** and press **Enter**.

    This step makes drive A the current drive.

11. Type **DIR** and press **Enter**.

    This step displays a directory listing of the contents of the disk in drive A so that you can verify that the copies were made.

Copy files to drive C

Use this same procedure to copy files from drive A to drive C. Start from drive A and then type **COPY *.* C:**.

REVIEW

To copy all files to a different drive

1. Insert a floppy disk into the drive.
2. Change to the directory that contains the files you want to copy.
3. Type **COPY *.* A:**. If you want to specify a different drive, type that drive name instead of A:.
4. Press **Enter**.

TASK

Rename a file

before

C:\DATA>RENAME AUTOEXEC.OLD AUTOEXEC.BAK

Oops!

If you see the message `Duplicate file name or file not found`, the new name you typed already exists or the original name did not exist. Try the command again.

1. Type **CD\DATA** and press **Enter**.

   This command tells DOS to change to the DATA directory. This directory contains the file you want to rename.

2. Type **RENAME**.

   You use the RENAME command to rename files.

3. Press the **space bar once**.

   Pressing the space bar once inserts a space between the command name and the next part of the command (the name of the file you want to rename).

4. Type **AUTOEXEC.OLD**.

   AUTOEXEC.OLD is the name of the file you want to rename. If you do not have this file, type the name of one you do have.

5. Press the **space bar once**.

   Pressing the space bar once inserts a space between the file name and the next part of the command (the new name you want to assign the file).

6. Type **AUTOEXEC.BAK**.

   AUTOEXEC.BAK is the new name you want to assign the file.

after

```
C:\DATA>RENAME AUTOEXEC.OLD AUTOEXEC.BAK

C:\DATA>DIR

 Volume in drive C is HARD DISK
 Volume Serial Number is 1724-0637
 Directory of C:\DATA

.            <DIR>     09-04-91  12:39a
..           <DIR>     09-04-91  12:39a
AUTOEXEC BAK        98 09-04-91  12:49a
AUTOEXEC BAT        98 09-04-91  12:49a
Q        BAT       128 08-28-91  12:01a
WS4      BAT       128 08-28-91  12:02a
        6 file(s)        452 bytes
                     2220032 bytes free

C:\DATA>
```

7. Press **Enter**.

   Pressing Enter confirms the command. The file named AUTOEXEC.OLD is now named AUTOEXEC.BAK.

8. Type **DIR** and press **Enter**.

   This step displays a directory listing so that you can verify the file was renamed.

Rename a group of files

You also can rename a group of files. For step 4 of the TASK section, use wild cards to specify the files you want to rename. For step 6 of the TASK section, use wild cards to specify the names for the new files. For instance, RENAME *.DOC *.TXT renames all files with a DOC extension to files with a TXT extension.

REVIEW

To rename a file

1. Change to the directory that contains the file you want to rename.
2. Type **RENAME**.
3. Press the **space bar once**.
4. Type the name of the file you want to rename. (You can use wild cards to specify a group of files.)
5. Press the **space bar once**.
6. Type the new name you want to assign the file. (If you specified a group of files for step 4, you can use wild cards to specify the new name of a group of files.)
7. Press **Enter**.

TASK

Delete a file

before

Oops!

If you see the message `File not found`, the file name that you typed does not exist. Check your typing and try again.

1. **Type CD\DATA and press Enter.**

   This step tells DOS to change to the DATA directory. This directory contains the file you want to rename.

2. **Type DEL.**

   The DEL command tells DOS to delete a file.

3. **Press the space bar once.**

   Pressing the space bar once inserts a space between the command name and the next part of the command (the file name).

4. **Type AUTOEXEC.BAK.**

   AUTOEXEC.BAK is the name of the file you want to delete. If you don't have a file named AUTOEXEC.BAK, type the name of one that you do have. Be sure, however, that you want to delete the file.

5. **Press Enter.**

   Pressing Enter confirms the command. The file you specified is deleted.

6. **Type DIR and press Enter.**

   This step displays a directory listing so that you can verify the file was deleted.

after

```
C:\DATA>DEL AUTOEXEC.BAK

C:\DATA>DIR

 Volume in drive C is HARD DISK
 Volume Serial Number is 1724-0637
 Directory of C:\DATA

.            <DIR>     09-04-91  12:39a
..           <DIR>     09-04-91  12:39a
AUTOEXEC BAT        98 09-04-91  12:49a
Q        BAT       128 08-28-91  12:01a
WS4      BAT       128 08-28-91  12:02a
        5 file(s)        354 bytes
                     2195456 bytes free

C:\DATA>
```

Delete a group of files

You can delete a group of files by using wild cards for the file name in step 4 of the TASK section. To delete all files, see *TASK: Delete all files*.

REVIEW

To delete a file

1. Change to the directory that contains the file you want to delete.
2. Type **DEL**.
3. Press the **space bar once**.
4. Type the name of the file you want to delete.
5. Press **Enter**

Be careful!

It's easy to type **DEL** when you mean to type something else. Be sure to read all prompts carefully. Also, it's good practice to use the DIR command to review the file listing of the disk or directory before you delete a file.

Delete all files

before

```
A:\>DEL *.*
All files in directory will be deleted!
Are you sure (Y/N)?
```

Oops!

If you change your mind, type **N** in step 7 of the TASK section.

1. **Insert a disk into drive A.**

   Use the disk that you have used for other tasks. If you haven't been following other tasks, insert a disk that contains files you do not need. Don't insert a disk with files you want to save.

   If you need help inserting the disk, see *TASK: Insert a disk*.

2. **Type A: and press Enter.**

   This step tells DOS to switch to drive A. Drive A contains the files you want to delete.

   To delete files in a directory, change to that directory.

3. **Type DEL.**

   The DEL command tells DOS to delete a file.

4. **Press the space bar once.**

   Pressing the space bar once inserts a space between the command name and the next part of the command (the file name).

5. **Type *.*.**

   After the DEL command, you type the name of the file you want to delete. The wild cards used here (*.*) specify all files.

   Be sure that you want to delete all files.

after

```
A:\>DEL *.*
All files in directory will be deleted!
Are you sure (Y/N)?Y

A:\>DIR

 Volume in drive A is DATA DISK
 Volume Serial Number is 07E9-1C5B
 Directory of A:\

File not found

A:\>
```

6. **Press Enter.**

   Pressing Enter confirms the command. You see the message `All files in directory will be deleted! Are you sure (Y/N)?`

7. **Type Y.**

   Typing Y confirms the deletion. All files are deleted.

8. **Type DIR and press Enter.**

   This step displays a directory listing so that you can confirm that the files were deleted.

Be careful!

It's easy to type **DEL** when you mean to type something else. Be sure to read all prompts carefully. Also, it's good practice to use the DIR command to review the file listing of the disk or directory before you delete all the files.

REVIEW

To delete all files

1. Change to the drive or directory that contains the files you want to delete.
2. Type **DEL**.
3. Press the **space bar once**.
4. Type ***.***.
5. Press **Enter**.
6. Type **Y**.

TASK

Undelete a file

before

Oops!

Not all files can be undeleted. See *Using MS-DOS 6*, Special Edition, for more information on how DOS deletes and undeletes files.

1. **Insert a disk into drive A.**

   Use the disk that you have used for other tasks. If you haven't been following other tasks, insert a disk that contains files that have been deleted.

2. **Type A: and press Enter.**

   This step tells DOS to switch to drive A. Drive A contains the files you want to undelete.

   To undelete files in a directory, change to that directory for this step.

3. **Type UNDELETE and press Enter.**

   This command undeletes files and is only available with DOS 5 or 6. You see some information on-screen:

   Directory used

   File specifications

   Status of deletion tracking file

   Number of files deleted

   Number of files able to be recovered

   After this information, you see the first deleted file that DOS found. The file name, extension, size, date, and time are listed. The first character of the file name is replaced with a question mark.

   Following the file information is the prompt `Undelete (Y/N)?`

after

```
Using the MS-DOS directory.

     ?UTOEXEC OLD       98  9-04-91 12:49a  ...A  Undelete (Y/N)?Y
     Please type the first character for ?UTOEXEC.OLD: A

File successfully undeleted.

     ?UTOEXEC BAT       98  9-04-91 12:49a  ...A  Undelete (Y/N)?Y
     Please type the first character for ?UTOEXEC.BAT: A

File successfully undeleted.

     ?       BAT       128  8-28-91 12:01a  ...A  Undelete (Y/N)?Y
     Please type the first character for ?       .BAT: Q

File successfully undeleted.

     ?S4     BAT       128  8-28-91 12:02a  ...A  Undelete (Y/N)?Y
     Please type the first character for ?S4     .BAT: W

File successfully undeleted.

A:\>
```

4. Type **Y**.

This step tells DOS to undelete this file. You see the message `Please type the first character for ?UTOEXEC.BAT.`

5. Type **A**.

A is the first character of this file name. The file is undeleted, and you return to the DOS prompt. (If other files were deleted, you can undelete this also. Type Y to tell DOS to undelete the file; then type the first letter. The After screen shows other files being undeleted.)

Who can use UNDELETE?

The UNDELETE command is only available with DOS Versions 5 and 6.

Don't know first letter?

If you don't know the first letter of the file, assign any letter. Then after you see what the file contains, use the RENAME command to rename the file.

REVIEW

To undelete a file

1. Change to the drive or directory that contains the file or files you want to undelete.
2. Type **UNDELETE**.
3. Press **Enter**.
4. When the file you want to undelete is listed, type **Y**.
5. Type the first character of the file name.
6. Continue typing **Y** and the first character of the file name until all files are undeleted.

Protecting Your Files

This section includes the following tasks:

Start the Backup program

Configure the Backup program

Back up selected directories

Back up selected files

Restore files

Exit the Backup program

Scan for viruses

Tell DOS to scan for viruses automatically

Start the Backup program

before

Oops!

To exit the Backup program, see *TASK: Exit the Backup program.*

1. Type MSBACKUP.

This command starts the DOS Backup program. This program enables you to back up your entire disk or select only certain directories or files to back up. You also can control the backup method.

For complete information on the Backup program, see *Using MS-DOS 6,* Special Edition.

2. Press Enter.

If you are running the program for the first time, you are prompted to select the configuration. (For more information about selecting the configuration, see *TASK: Configure the Backup program.*)

If you have already configured the program, the main menu appears. You can choose to Backup, Restore, or Compare files.

after

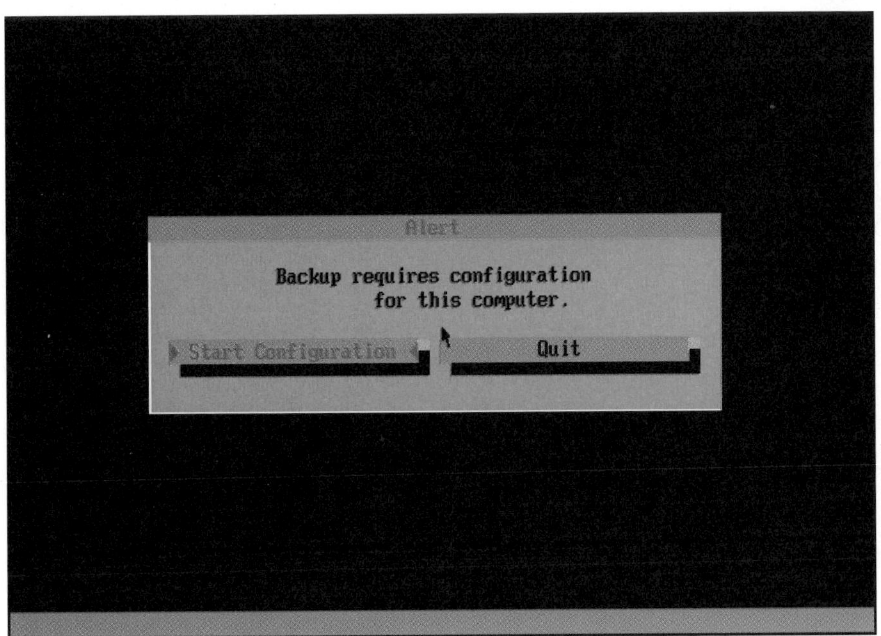

Use Microsoft Windows?

DOS 6 includes a Microsoft Windows version of the Backup program. See *Using MS-DOS 6,* Special Edition for help on this program.

REVIEW

1. Type **MSBACKUP**.
2. Press **Enter**.

To start the Backup program

What is a backup?

A *backup* is an extra set of the data and programs on your hard disk. If something happens to the original copy, you can use the backup to restore the data and programs.

Configure the Backup program

(Part 1 of 3)

before

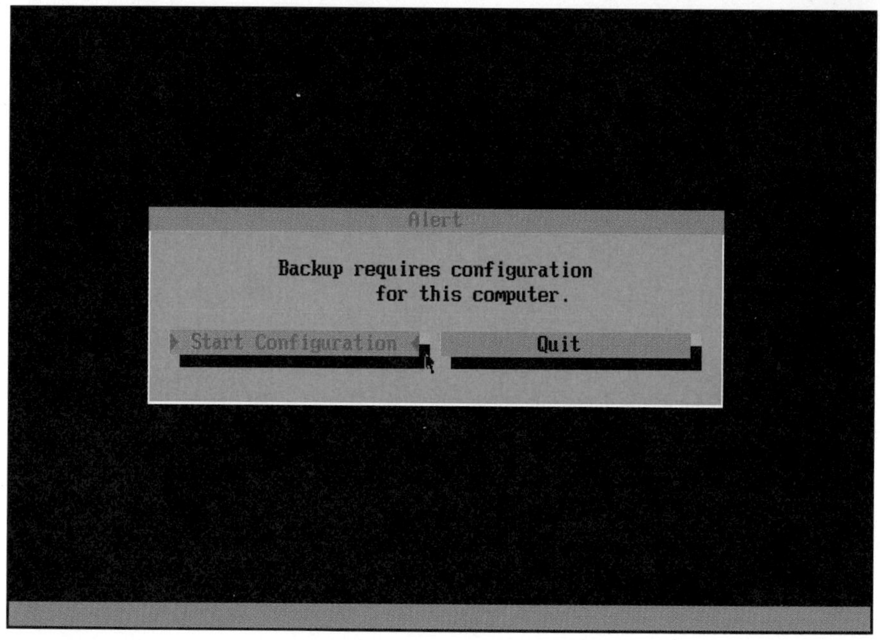

Oops!

If you don't want to do the configuration, select the Quit option. You can run the configuration program later. Until you complete the configuration, every time you use DOS Backup, DOS will remind you that you need to run the Floppy Drive Change Line Test.

This task consists of three parts. The first part, Start the configuration, is covered here. The next four pages explain the rest of the task.

1. When the alert box tells you that DOS Backup requires configuration, press **Enter**.

   This alert box appears the first time you run DOS Backup. Pressing Enter selects the Start Configuration option. You see options for the screen display and mouse. DOS Backup tries to determine the type of mouse and monitor you are using; generally the program guesses correctly.

2. Press **Enter**.

   This step accepts the defaults for the screen and mouse options. You are next prompted to perform the Floppy Drive Change Line Test. Performing this test ensures that DOS Backup can use the fastest and most reliable method of backing up.

3. Press **Enter**.

   This step starts the floppy drive test. The next screen lists the backup devices.

after

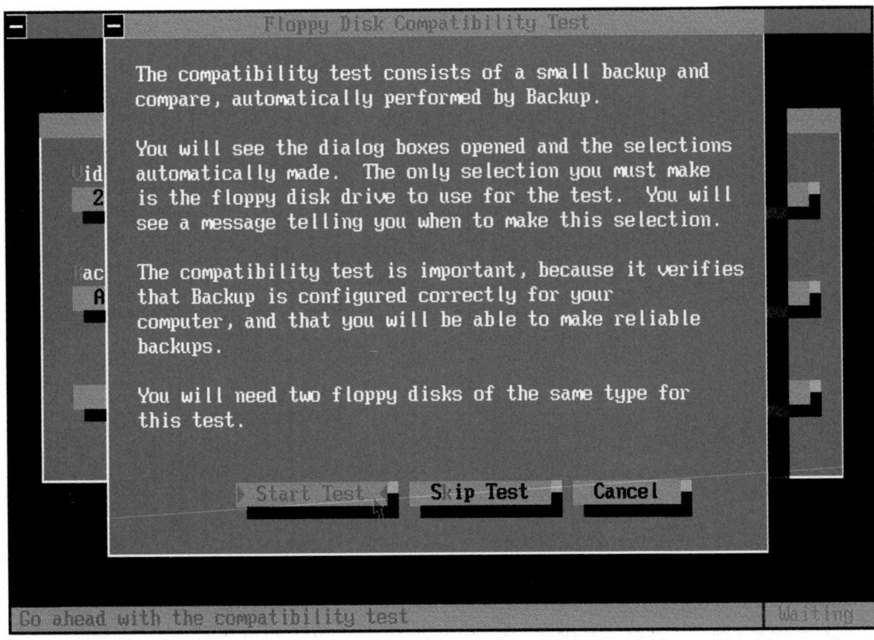

Floppy Disk Compatibility Test
The compatibility test consists of a small backup and compare, automatically performed by Backup.
You will see the dialog boxes opened and the selections automatically made. The only selection you must make is the floppy disk drive to use for the test. You will see a message telling you when to make this selection.
The compatibility test is important, because it verifies that Backup is configured correctly for your computer, and that you will be able to make reliable backups.
You will need two floppy disks of the same type for this test.
Start Test
Skip Test
Cancel
Go ahead with the compatibility test
Waiting

Need more information?

For complete configuration information, see *Using MS-DOS 6,* Special Edition.

4. Press **Enter**.

   This step accepts the default backup devices. DOS Backup tests the CPU speed, reads the hard drive, and displays a performance index. You are next prompted for a Floppy Disk Compatibility Test.

   Turn the page to continue configuring DOS Backup.

REVIEW

To configure the Backup program

1. When the Alert box appears, press **Enter** to start the configuration.
2. Change any screen display and mouse options; then press **Enter**.
3. Press **Enter** to start the floppy drive test.
4. Press **Enter** to accept the default backup devices.

Configure the Backup program

(Part 2 of 3)

before

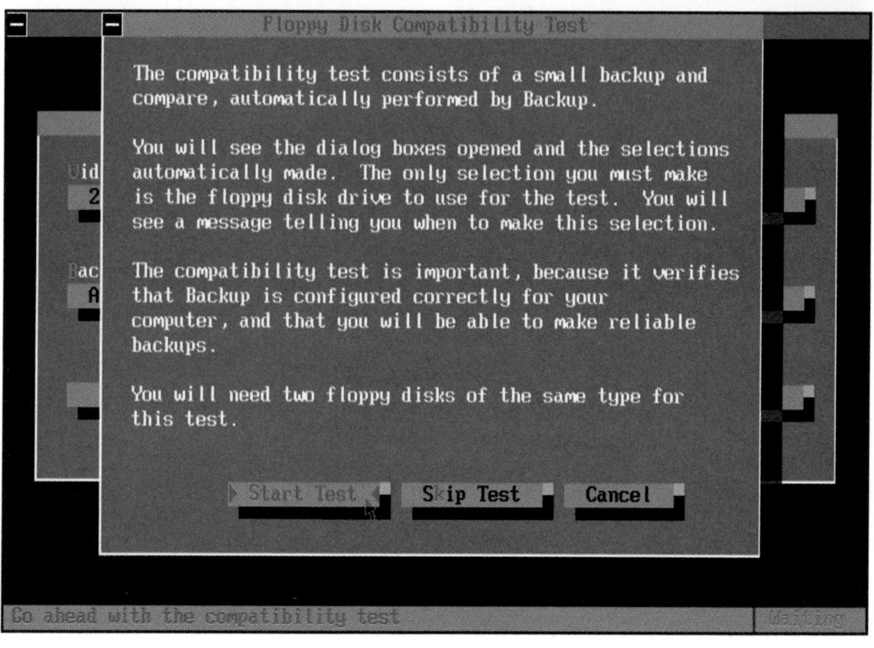

Oops!

To skip the test, select Skip Test for step 1.

This task consists of three parts. The first part is covered on the preceding two pages. These two pages cover the second part. Turn the page for the conclusion of this task.

1. When DOS asks you whether you want to run the compatibility test, press **Enter**.

   This step starts the test. The Backup program goes through a backup routine, selecting the appropriate options and test files. You see a message stating that the test will be paused so that you can select the backup device.

2. Press **Enter**.

   This step clears the message.

   DOS prompts you to select the device (floppy drive) that you want to back up to. The default, drive A, is selected.

3. Press **Enter**.

   This step accepts the default drive—drive A—as the device that you will back up to. DOS then prompts you to insert a floppy disk. (The After screen shows this step.)

after

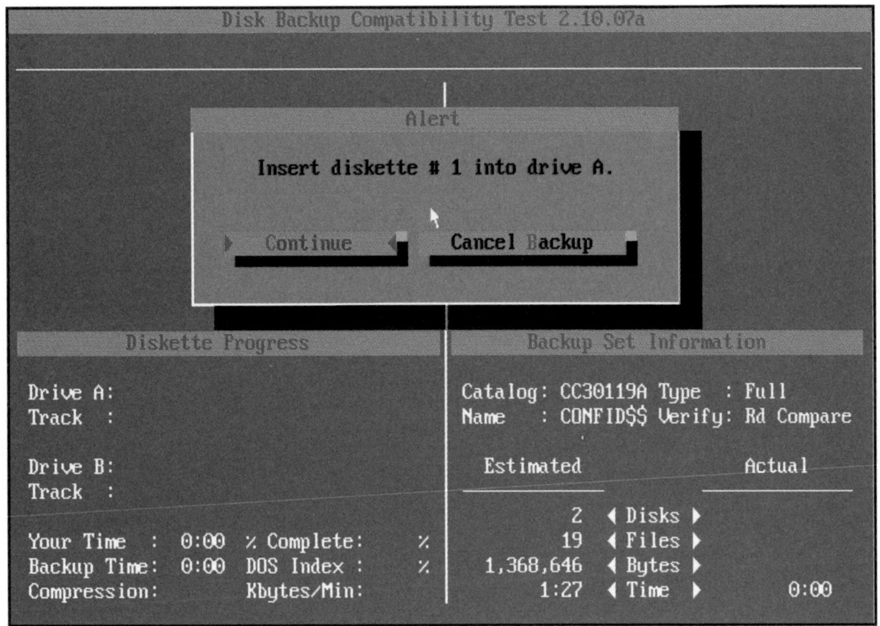

4. Insert a floppy disk and press **Enter**.

   Be sure that you insert a blank disk. If you insert a disk that contains information, the information will be overwritten. (DOS does, however, warn you before overwriting the information.)

   The backup process begins. When the first disk you inserted is filled with information, DOS prompts you to insert another disk.

Receive an error message?

If you receive any error messages, see *Using MS-DOS 6,* Special Edition, for help.

REVIEW

To configure the Backup program

1. Press **Enter** to start the test.
2. Press **Enter** to continue.
3. Press **Enter** to accept the default drive.
4. Insert the first disk and press **Enter**.

Configure the Backup program

(Part 3 of 3)

before

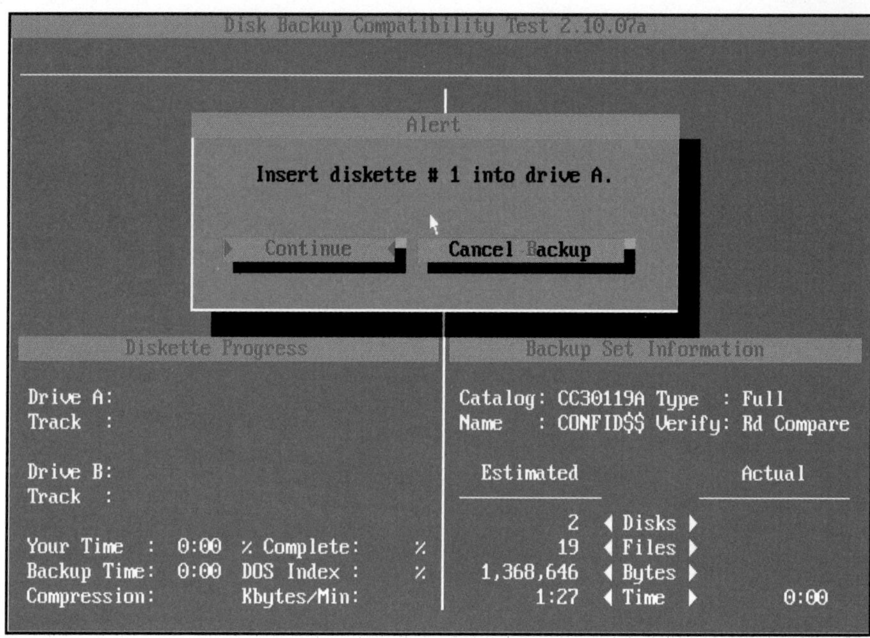

This task consists of three parts. The preceding four pages explained the beginning of the process. These two pages conclude the process.

1. Eject the first disk, insert another disk, and press **Enter**.

   This step continues the backup process. You see the progress of the backup on-screen. A message appears telling you that the backup is complete.

2. Press **Enter**.

   This step clears the message and starts the compare process. (The *compare process* compares the backup information to the original information to make sure that the backup copy is accurate.) You are prompted to insert disk 1.

3. Insert disk 1 and press **Enter**.

   The compare process starts. DOS then prompts you to insert disk 2.

4. Insert disk 2 and press **Enter**.

   You see a message that says the compare process is complete.

5. Press **Enter**.

   You see a message that says the test was successful.

Oops!

If you accidentally insert a disk that contains information you want to save, eject the disk, insert another disk, and press Enter.

after

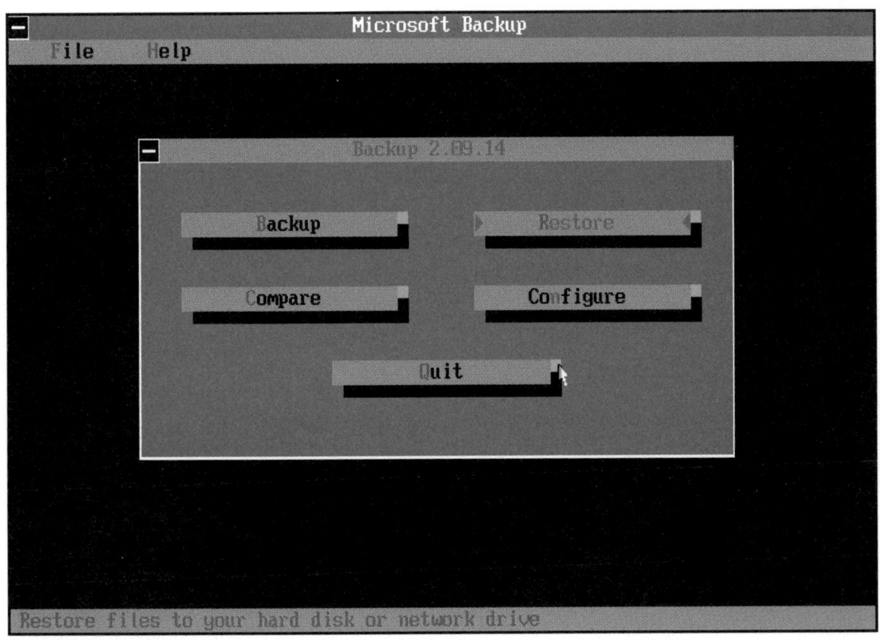

6. Press **Enter**.

   This step saves the configuration and returns you to the main menu.

Run the test later

If you configured the program previously but did not run the test, you can run the test at any time. To do so, select Configure from the main menu. Then select Compatibility test and run the test.

REVIEW

To configure the Backup program

1. Eject the first disk, insert the second disk, and press **Enter**.
2. Press **Enter** to start the compare.
3. Insert disk 1 and press **Enter**.
4. Insert disk 2 and press **Enter**.
5. Press **Enter** to end the compare.
6. Press **Enter** to return to the main menu.

Back up selected directories

(Part 1 of 2)

before

Oops!

To return to the Backup screen, click on the Cancel button.

Backing up selected directories is a two-part process. These two pages cover the first part. Turn the page for the second part.

1. **Start the Backup program.**

   For help with this task, see *TASK: Start the Backup program.*

2. **From the main menu, press Enter.**

   Pressing Enter selects the first choice on the main menu, Backup, which is highlighted. You see the Backup screen. Certain options are preset, depending on your configuration. By default, the default set is used, drive C is the drive to be backed up, drive A is the drive to back up to, and the full method is used.

3. **Type 1.**

   This step selects the Select Files option. You have to specify the files to back up. You see a directory listing on the left side of the screen and a file listing on the right.

after

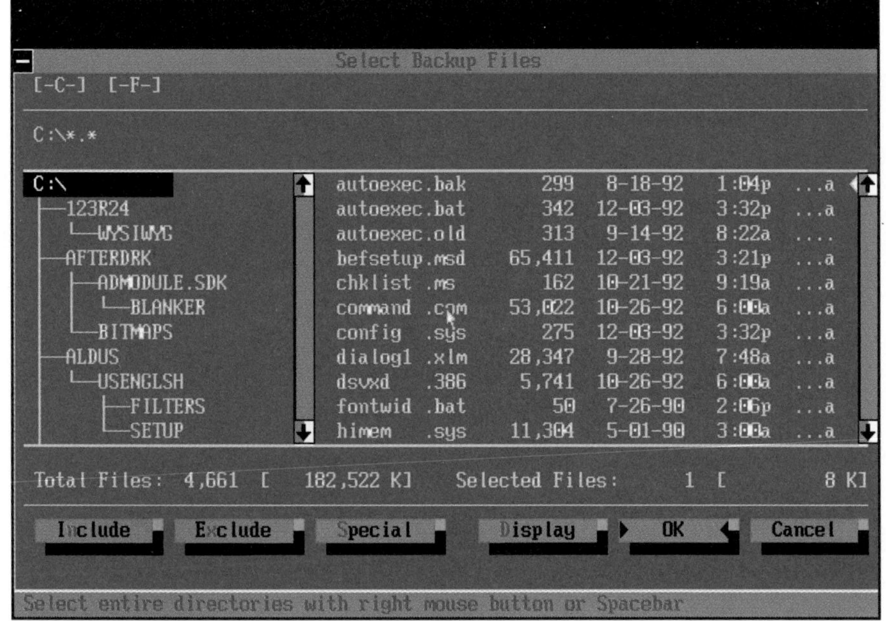

Need more information?

For more information on the backup process, see Using *MS-DOS 6,* Special Edition.

REVIEW

To back up selected directories

1. Start the Backup program.
2. From the main menu, select **Backup**.
3. Type **1** to select Select Files.

Back up selected directories

(Part 2 of 2)

before

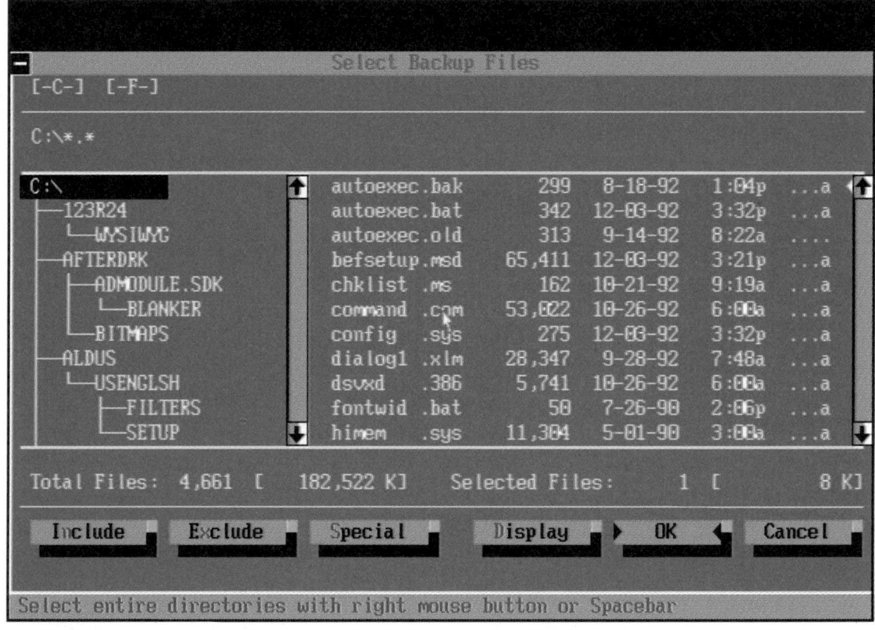

Oops!

To cancel the backup, select Cancel before step 5 in the TASK section.

Backing up selected directories is a two-part process. The preceding two pages cover the first part. These two pages cover the second part.

1. Press the ↓ key to highlight the DATA directory.

   This step selects the directory that you want to back up. If you don't have this directory, select one you do have.

2. Press the **space bar**.

   This step marks the directory to be backed up. The directory has an arrow next to it, and all files in the file list have a check mark next to them. These symbols indicate that the directory and all files are selected.

3. Press **Enter**.

   This step confirms your backup selections and returns you to the Backup screen. DOS Backup calculates the number of disks you will need and the total size of all selected files.

4. Type **S**.

   This step selects the Start Backup button. You are prompted to insert a disk.

after

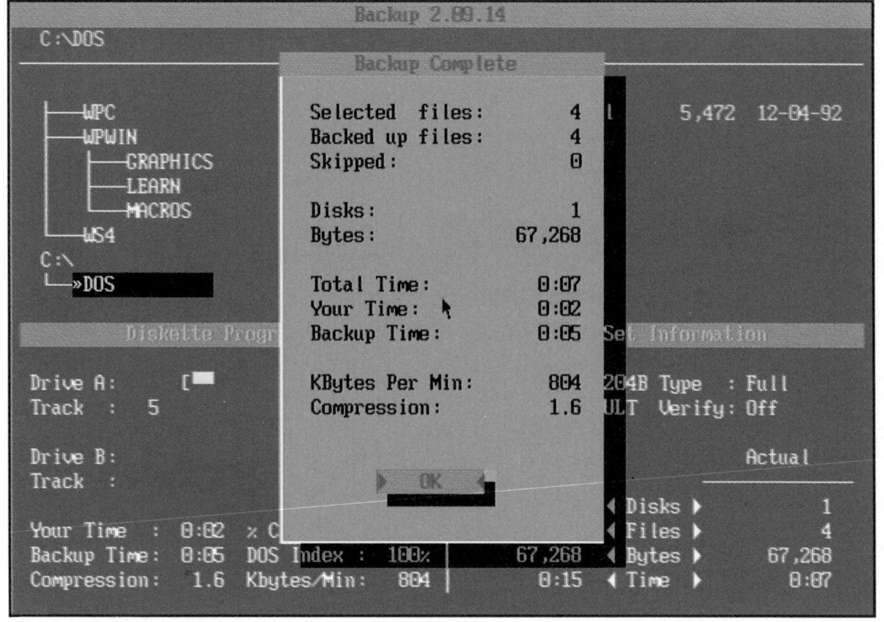

5. Insert the disk and press **Enter**.

   You may be prompted to insert additional disks. If so, insert the disk and press Enter. When all files have been backed up, you see a message that reads `Backup Complete`. The After screen shows this step.

6. Press **Enter**.

   This step returns you to the main menu. To exit the Backup program, see *TASK: Exit the Backup program*.

Label the disks

Clearly label the disks that you use in numerical order—for example, Backup disk 1, Backup disk 2, and so on. You will need to restore the information in the same order you backed it up.

REVIEW

To back up selected directories

1. Highlight the first directory you want to back up.
2. Press the **space bar**.
3. Repeat steps 4 and 5 for all directories you want to back up.
4. Press **Enter** when you finish selecting directories.
5. Type **S** to start the backup.
6. Insert disks and press **Enter** as prompted.

Restore files

See *TASK: Restore files* for help restoring backup files.

Back up selected files

(Part 1 of 2)

before

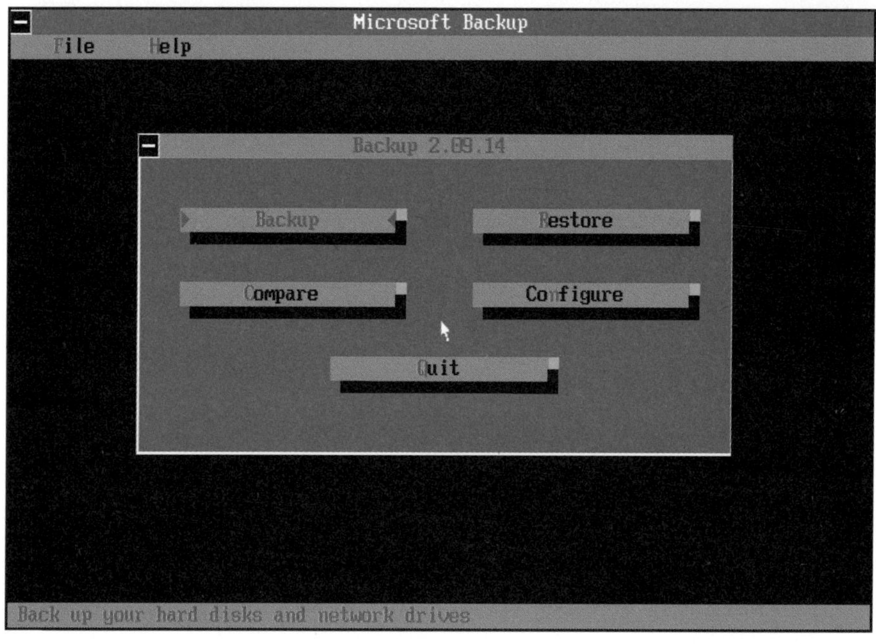

Oops!

To return to the Backup screen, click on the Cancel button.

Backing up selected files is a two-part process. These two pages cover the first part of the process. Turn the page for the second part.

1. Start the Backup program.

   For help with this task, see *TASK: Start the Backup program*.

2. From the main menu, press **Enter**.

   By default the first choice, Backup, is selected. Pressing Enter selects this option. You see the Backup screen. Certain options are preset, depending on your configuration. By default, the default set is used, drive C is the drive to be backed up, drive A is the drive to back up to, and the full method is used.

3. Type **1**.

   This step selects the Select Files option. You have to specify the files to back up. You see a directory listing on the left of the screen and a file listing on the right.

after

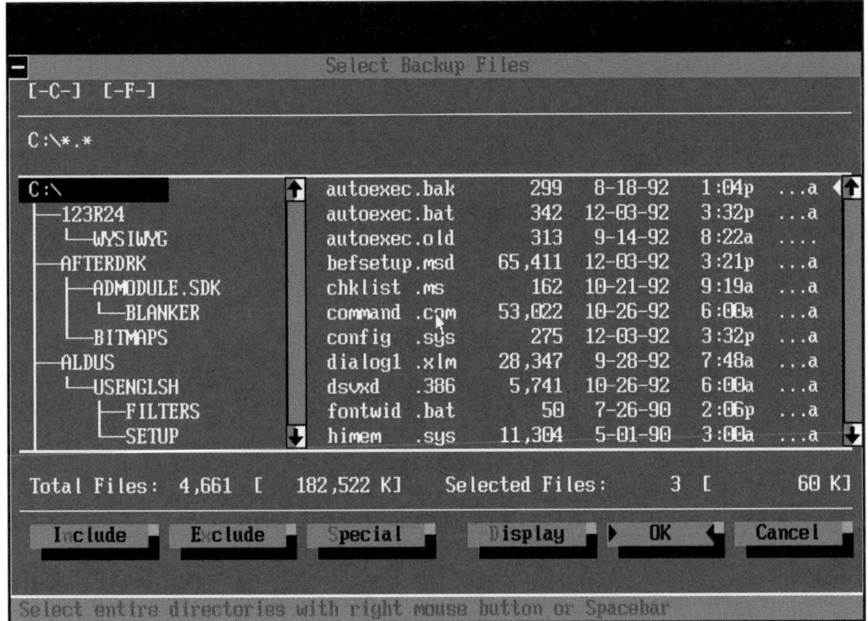

Restore files

See *TASK: Restore files* for help restoring the backup files.

REVIEW

To back up selected files

1. Start the Backup program.
2. From the main menu, select **Backup**.
3. Type **1** to select Select Files.

Back up selected files

(Part 2 of 2)

before

```
Select Backup Files
[-C-] [-F-]

C:\*.*

C:\                   autoexec.bak      299   8-18-92  1:04p ...a
 ├─123R24             autoexec.bat      342  12-03-92  3:32p ...a
 │ └─WYSIWYG          autoexec.old      313   9-14-92  8:22a ....
 ├─AFTERDRK           befsetup.msd   65,411  12-03-92  3:21p ...a
 │ ├─ADMODULE.SDK     chklist .ms       162  10-21-92  9:19a ...a
 │ │ └─BLANKER        command .com   53,022  10-26-92  6:00a ...a
 │ └─BITMAPS          config  .sys      275  12-03-92  3:32p ...a
 ├─ALDUS              dialog1 .xlm   28,347   9-28-92  7:48a ...a
 │ └─USENGLSH         dsvxd   .386    5,741  10-26-92  6:00a ...a
 │   ├─FILTERS        fontwid .bat       50   7-26-90  2:06p ...a
 │   └─SETUP          himem   .sys   11,304   5-01-90  3:00a ...a

Total Files:  4,661 [   182,522 K]   Selected Files:      3 [       60 K]

 Include   Exclude   Special    Display    OK    Cancel

Select entire directories with right mouse button or Spacebar
```

Oops!

To cancel the backup, select Cancel before step 7 of the Task section.

Backing up selected directories is a two-part process. The preceding two pages cover the first part. These two pages cover the second part.

1. Press the ↓ key to highlight the Excel directory.

   This step selects the directory that contains the file you want to back up. The files in this directory appear in the right side of the window. If you have already backed up files, these files might already be selected. To unselect a file or directory, press the space bar to remove the arrow or check mark.

2. Press the → key to move to the file listing.

   This step moves the cursor to the file listing.

3. Press the ↓ key to highlight the BOOKS.XLS file.

   This step marks the file to be backed up. If you don't have this file, select one that you do have.

4. Press the **space bar**.

   This step places a check mark next to the file. (***Note:*** If the file already has a check mark next to it, skip this step.)

5. Press **Enter**.

   This step confirms your backup selections and returns you to the backup screen. DOS Backup calculates the number of disks you will need and the total size of all selected files.

after

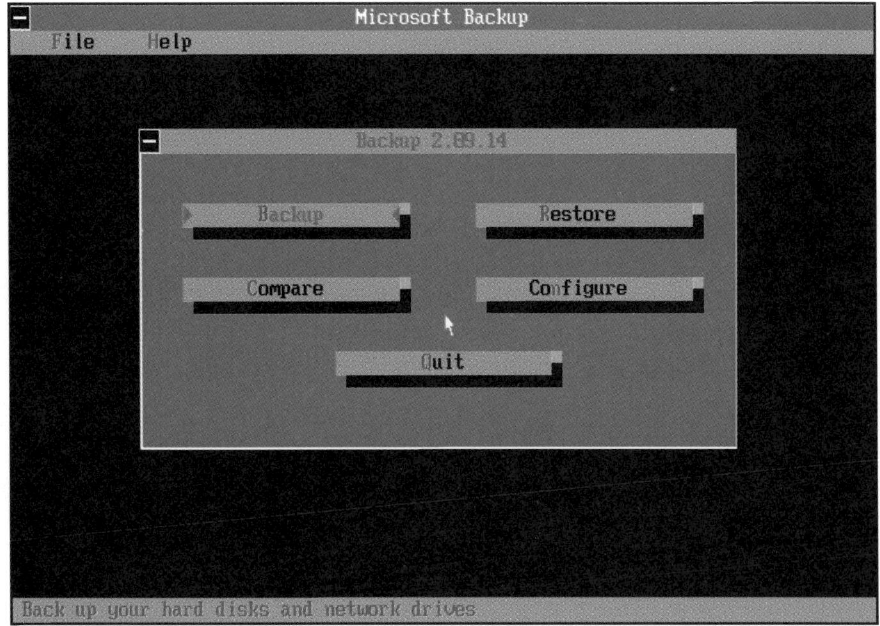

6. Type **S**.

   This step selects the Start Backup button. You are prompted to insert a disk.

7. Insert the disk and press **Enter**.

   When all files have been backed up, you see a message that reads `Backup Complete`.

8. Press **Enter**.

   This step returns you to the main menu. To exit the Backup program, see *TASK: Exit the Backup program*.

Select more than one file

You can select more than one file. Follow the same procedure to mark all the files you want to back up.

Other files selected?

If other files were selected previously—the last time you ran Backup—those files will be backed up as well. To exclude those files, deselect them. (For information, see Using *MS-DOS 6,* Special Edition.)

REVIEW

To back up selected files

1. Use the ↓ key to highlight the directory that contains the first file you want to back up.
2. Press the → key to move to the file listing.
3. Use the ↓ key to select the file.
4. Press the **space bar**.
5. Repeat steps 4 through 7 for all directories you want to back up. Then press **Enter**
6. Type **S** to start the backup.
7. Insert disks and press **Enter** as prompted.

Restore files

before

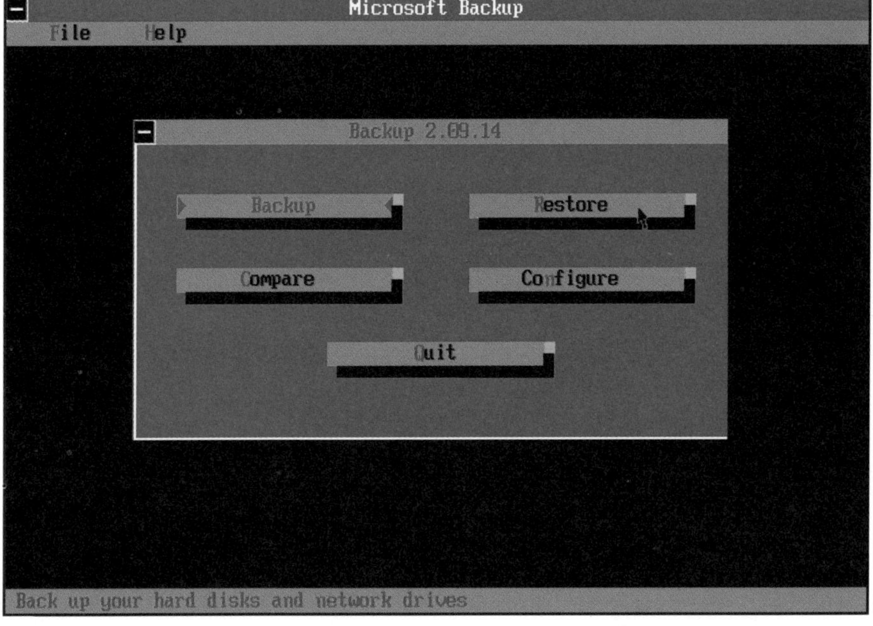

Oops!

To quit the restore, select Cancel from the Restore screen.

1. Start the Backup program.

   For help with this step, see *TASK: Start the Backup program*.

2. Type **R**.

   This step selects the Restore option.

3. Type **i**.

   This step selects the Restore Files option.

4. Press the **space bar**.

   This step selects all files.

5. Press **Alt-S**.

   This step starts the restore process. You are prompted to insert the backup disk.

6. Insert backup disk 1 and press **Enter**.

   This step tells DOS to restore the files on the backup disk you've inserted. If the backup set contains several disks, you will be prompted for each disk. Insert the appropriate disks as prompted. When the restore is complete, you see a message that reads `Restore complete`.

7. Press **Enter**.

   This step finishes the restore and returns you to the main menu.

after

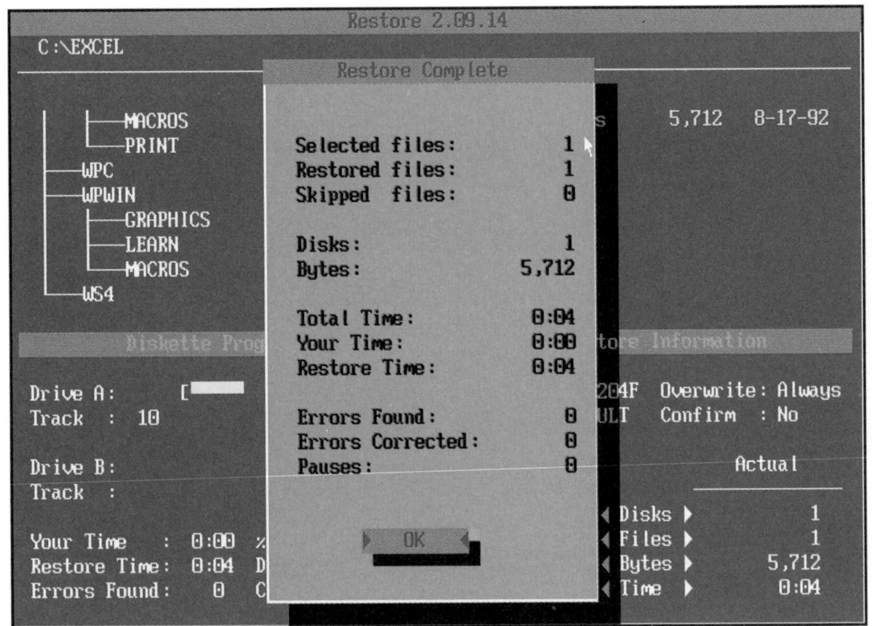

Exit the Backup program

See *TASK: Exit the Backup program* for help on exiting.

REVIEW

To restore files

1. Start the Backup program.
2. Type **R** to select the Restore option.
3. Type **i** to select the Restore Files option.
4. Press the **space bar** to select all files.
5. Press **Alt-S** to start the restore.
6. Insert the backup disks and press **Enter** as prompted.
7. Press **Enter**.

Why Restore?

Backed up files are stored in a special format that DOS cannot read directly. In order to use those files, you must run them through the restore process, which makes the files readable.

TASK

Exit the Backup program

before

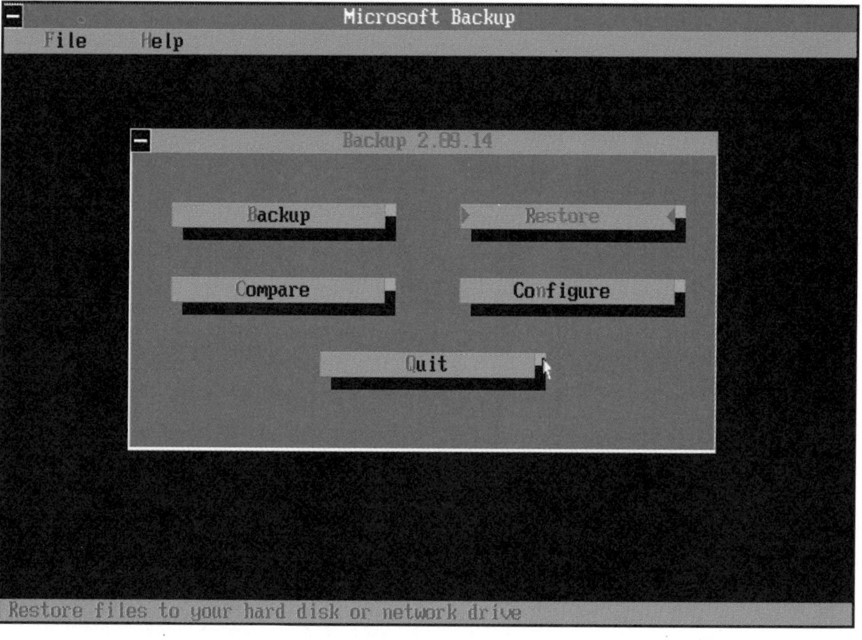

From the Backup main menu, type Q.

This step selects the Quit command. You return to the DOS prompt.

Oops!

If you aren't at the Backup main menu, press Esc until the menu appears.

after

Start the Backup program

See *TASK: Start the Backup program* for help starting the program.

REVIEW

To exit the Backup program

From the Backup main menu, type **Q**.

Scan for viruses

before

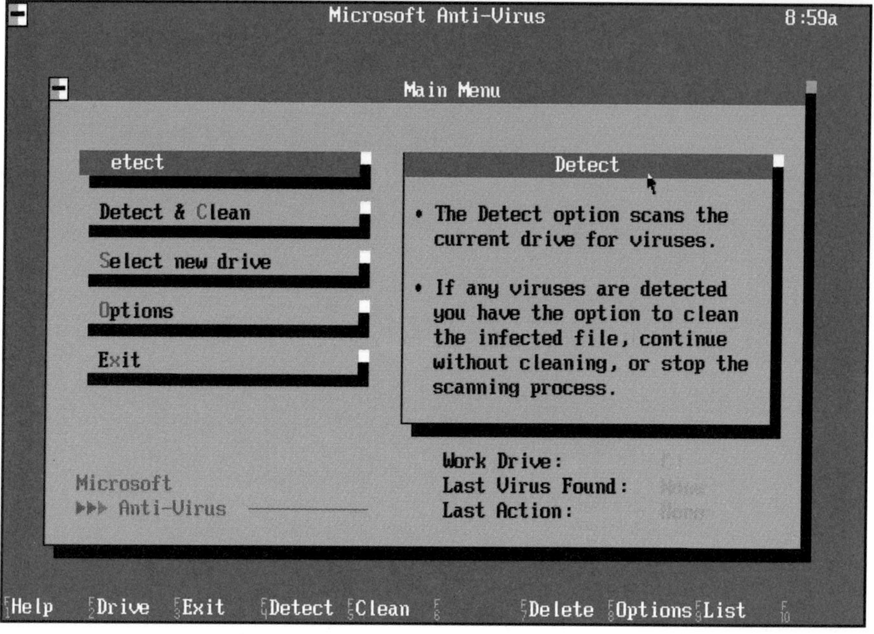

Oops!

To cancel the virus scan, select Exit for step 3 of the Task section.

1. Type **MSAV**.

   This command starts the anti-virus program used to detect and remove viruses. This program is available only with Version 6 of DOS.

2. Press **Enter**.

   This step executes the command. You see the main menu , which contains options that enable you to detect a virus, detect a virus and clean the disk, select a drive, set options, and exit. The Detect option is selected. The Before screen shows this step.

   For complete information on all options, see *Using MS-DOS 6,* Special Edition.

3. Press **Enter**.

   This step selects the Detect option. The anti-virus program scans memory for viruses, and then checks directories and files. (The scan may take some time.) When the scan is complete, you see a report of what was found—what was checked, infected, and cleaned.

4. Press **Enter**.

   This step closes the report. You return to the main menu.

after

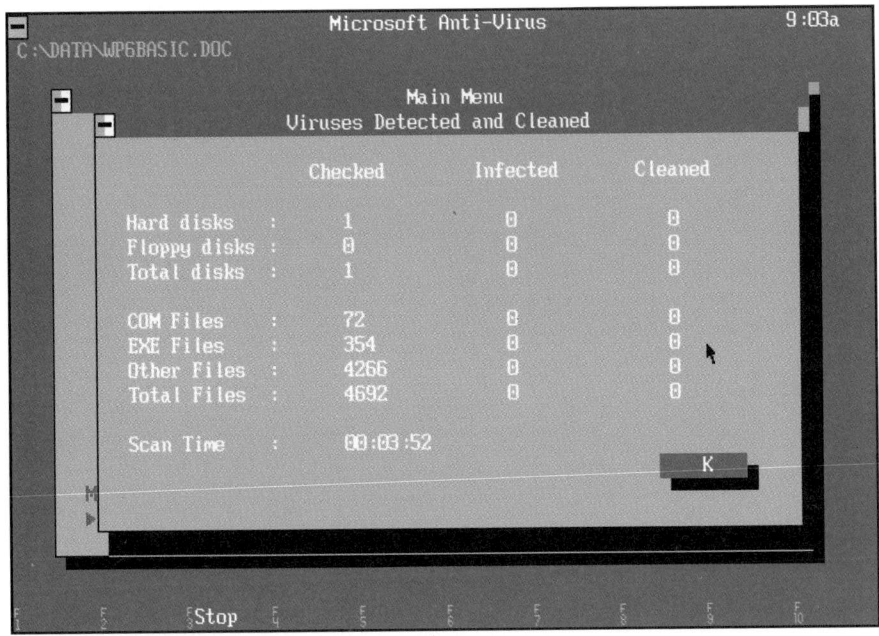

5. Type **x**.

   This step selects the Exit option. A message appears prompting you to confirm that you want to exit.

6. Press **Enter**.

   This step closes the anti-virus program. You return to the DOS prompt.

Found a virus?

If the program finds a virus, call a technical support representative for help. Or see *Using MS-DOS 6,* Special Edition, for information.

REVIEW

To scan for viruses

1. Type **MSAV**.
2. Press **Enter**.
3. Select the option you want.
4. Press **Enter**.
5. After reading the results, press **Enter**.
6. Type **x**.
7. Press **Enter**.

Use Microsoft Windows?

Included with DOS 6 is a Windows version of the anti-virus program. See *Using MS-DOS 6,* Special Edition, for help using this program.

TASK

Tell DOS to scan for viruses automatically

before

Oops!

To unload the program, press the Alt-V key combination, and then press the Alt-U key combination.

1. **Type VSAFE.**

   This command loads a terminate-and-stay-resident (TSR) program that checks for viruses. (A TSR is a program that is loaded into memory and stays there. You can then access the program at any time by pressing a special key combination.)

2. **Press Enter.**

   This step executes the command. The program is now loaded into memory. A message appears telling you that the installation was complete; you return to the DOS prompt.

   The program will do the following:

   - Warn you if a virus tries to format the hard disk.
   - Check all executable (EXE) files as they are executed.
   - Check the boot sector for viruses.
   - Protect the boot sector.

after

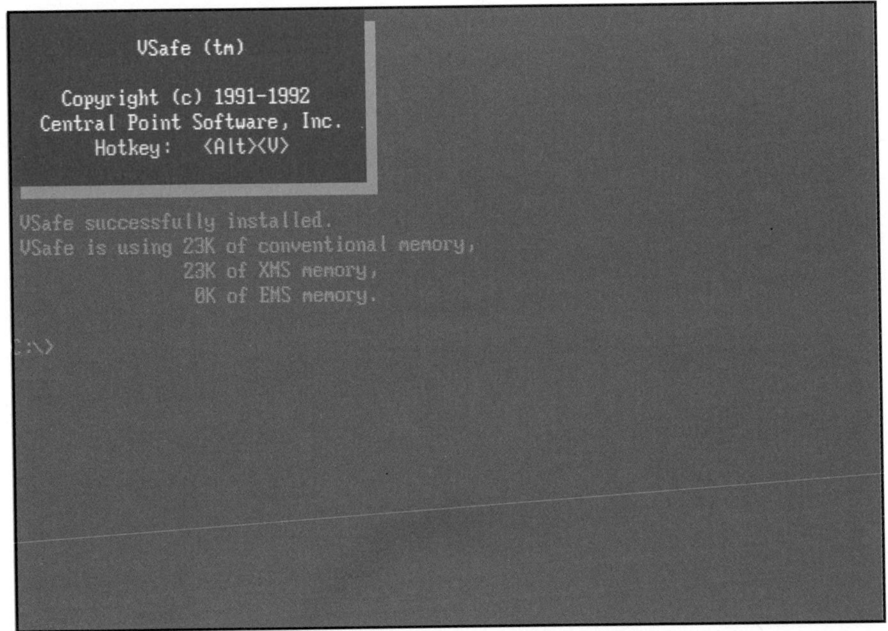

VSafe (tm)
Copyright (c) 1991-1992
Central Point Software, Inc.
Hotkey: <Alt><V>
VSafe successfully installed.
VSafe is using 23K of conventional memory,
23K of XMS memory,
0K of EMS memory.
C:\>

Add to AUTOEXEC.BAT

You must run this program every time you turn on the computer. If you want to set up the program so that you don't have to load it every time you turn on the computer, add the VSAFE program to your AUTOEXEC.BAT file. See *Using MS-DOS 6,* Special Edition, for help with this task.

REVIEW

1. Type **VSAFE**.
2. Press **Enter**.

To tell DOS to scan for viruses auto-matically

Change settings

To change the settings, press Alt-V to access the menu. For information on the settings, see *Using MS-DOS 6,* Special Edition.

Customizing and Optimizing Your Computer

This section covers the following tasks:

Display a volume label

Change a volume label

Check the DOS version

Check disk space and memory

Set the date

Set the time

Set the path

Check memory information

Optimize memory

Defragment a disk

TASK

Display a volume label

before

Oops!

If you see the message `Bad command or file name`, you typed the command incorrectly. Try again.

1. **Type VOL.**

   VOL is the volume command. *Volume* is another name for *drive*.

2. **Press Enter.**

   Pressing Enter confirms the command. You see the volume label (which is the volume name) assigned to the disk. You also see the volume serial number.

after

```
C:\>VOL

 Volume in drive C is HARD DISK
 Volume Serial Number is 1724-0637

C:\>
```

REVIEW

To display a volume label

1. Type **VOL**.
2. Press **Enter**.

TASK

Change a volume label

before

```
C:\>LABEL
Volume in drive C is HARD DISK
Volume Serial Number is 1724-0637
Volume label (11 characters, ENTER for none)?
```

Oops!

If you decide not to change the volume label, follow this same procedure to change the label back to its original name.

1. **Type LABEL.**

   LABEL is the label command. You use this command to change the volume label for the disk.

2. **Press Enter.**

   Pressing Enter confirms the command. You see the volume label (which is the name) currently assigned to the disk and the volume serial number. You also see the prompt `Volume label (11 characters, ENTER for none)?`

3. **Type SEO'S DISK.**

   SEO'S DISK is the new volume label you want to use.

4. **Press Enter.**

   Pressing Enter confirms the new volume label.

5. **Type VOL and press Enter.**

   This step verifies that the volume label has been changed. You see the volume label listed as `SEO'S DISK`.

after

```
C:\>LABEL
Volume in drive C is HARD DISK
Volume Serial Number is 1724-0637
Volume label (11 characters, ENTER for none)? SEO'S DISK

C:\>VOL

 Volume in drive C is SEO'S DISK
 Volume Serial Number is 1724-0637

C:\>
```

Does an error message appear?

If you see the message `Bad command or file name`, you typed the command incorrectly. Try again.

REVIEW

To change a volume label

1. Type **LABEL**.
2. Press **Enter**.
3. Type the label (up to 11 characters). You can include spaces in the label.
4. Press **Enter**.

TASK

Check the DOS version

before

Oops!

If you see the message `Bad command or file name`, you typed the command incorrectly. Try again.

1. Type **VER**.

   VER is the version command. You use this command to display the current DOS version.

2. Press **Enter**.

   Pressing Enter confirms the command. You see the current DOS version number. The After screen shows the current version as MS-DOS Version 6.00. Your version will be different from the one that appears in the After screen if you use a different DOS version.

after

C:\>VER
MS-DOS Version 5.00
C:\>

Why check DOS version?

Some programs require a certain version of DOS. Also, when you experience hardware or software problems and call for assistance, you may need to know the DOS version so that the problem can be remedied more quickly.

REVIEW

1. Type **VER**.
2. Press **Enter**.

To check the DOS version

TASK

Check disk space and memory

before

Oops!

If you see the message `Bad command or file name`, you typed the command incorrectly. Try typing it again.

1. Type **CHKDSK**.

   CHKDSK is the checkdisk command. You use this command to display some basic information about the disk.

2. Press **Enter**.

   Pressing Enter confirms the command. DOS checks the disk and displays information in three sections. The first section displays the following information:

   total disk space (in bytes)

   number of hidden files (and number of bytes)

   number of directories (and number of bytes)

   number of user files (and number of bytes)

   number of bad sectors if any (in bytes)

   number of bytes available on disk

   Remember that about 1 million bytes equals one megabyte (M). So if the display shows `1998848`, that number would equal about 2M.

after

```
C:\>CHKDSK

Volume SEO'S DISK  created 09-04-1991 12:52a
Volume Serial Number is 1724-0637

  21323776 bytes total disk space
    147456 bytes in 5 hidden files
    147456 bytes in 18 directories
  19030016 bytes in 601 user files
   1998848 bytes available on disk

      8192 bytes in each allocation unit
      2603 total allocation units on disk
       244 available allocation units on disk

    655360 total bytes memory
    491488 bytes free

C:\>
```

Other uses of CHKDSK

The CHKDSK command also lets you repair damage to the data structure. If you see any error messages after using this command, consult *Using MS-DOS 6*, Special Edition, for more information.

The middle section displays information about how space is allocated (assigned). See *Using MS-DOS 6*, Special Edition, for information on these lines.

The last section displays the following information about memory:

total bytes memory

total bytes free

Remember that roughly 1 thousand bytes equals one kilobyte (K). So if the display shows `655360`, that number would equal about 640K.

REVIEW

To check disk space and memory

1. Type **CHKDSK**.
2. Press **Enter**.

TASK

Set the date

before

Oops!

To restore the original date, use this same procedure and type the original date when you are prompted.

1. Type **DATE**.

   DATE is the command that you use to set the date.

2. Press **Enter**.

   Pressing Enter confirms the command. You see the prompt `Current date is`, followed by the current date. You also see the prompt `Enter new date (mm-dd-yy):`.

3. Type **02-13-93**.

   This is the new date you want to enter.

4. Press **Enter**.

   Pressing Enter confirms the new date.

after

```
C:\>DATE
Current date is Wed 09-04-1991
Enter new date (mm-dd-yy): 01-01-92

C:\>
```

Enter correct date and time

Your computer uses the date and time to keep track of when you save files to disk. Be sure that you enter the correct date and time so that your file information is accurate.

REVIEW

To set the date

1. Type **DATE**.
2. Press **Enter**.
3. Type the new date.
4. Press **Enter**.

Is the date set automatically?

Your computer may set the date automatically. If so, this task isn't necessary.

TASK

Set the time

before

1. **Type TIME.**

   TIME is the command that you use to set and display the time.

2. **Press Enter.**

   Pressing Enter confirms the command. You see the prompt `Current time is`, followed by the current time. You also see the prompt `Enter new time:`.

3. **Type 14:00:00.**

   This is the new time you want to set.

4. **Press Enter.**

   Pressing Enter confirms the new time.

Oops!

To restore the original time, use this same procedure and type the original time when you are prompted.

after

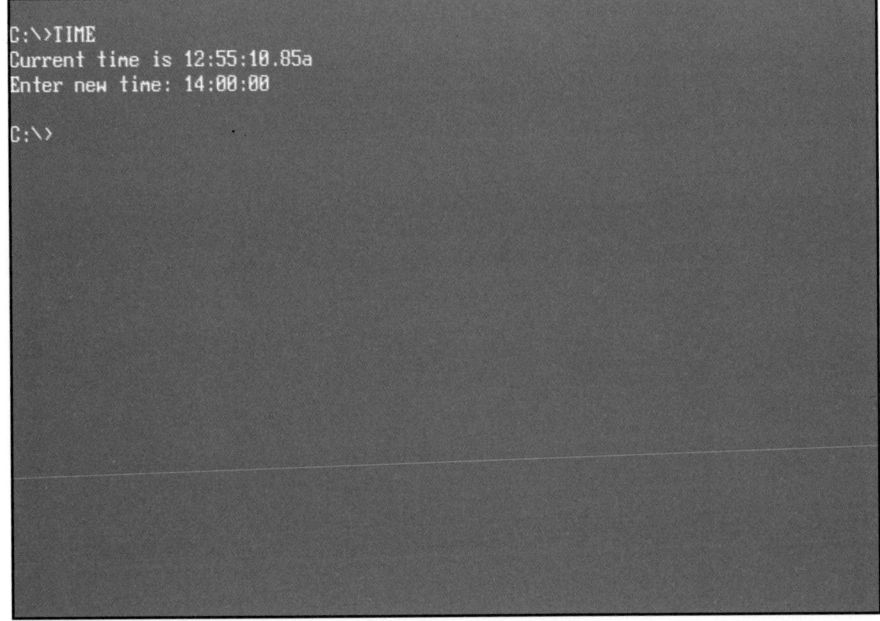
C:\>TIME
Current time is 12:55:10.85a
Enter new time: 14:00:00
C:\>

Use a different format

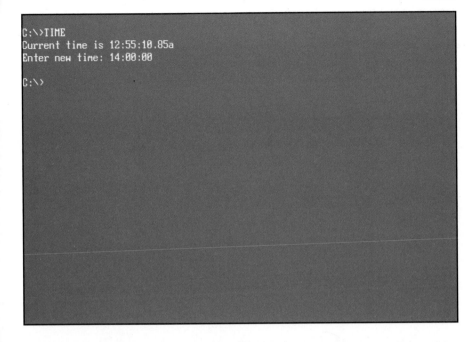

DOS Versions 4, 5, and 6 don't require that you enter military time. You can enter 2:00 PM as **2:00p**, for example.

REVIEW

To set the time

1. Type TIME.
2. Press Enter.
3. Type the new time.
4. Press Enter.

Is the time set automatically?

Your computer may automatically set the time. If so, this task may not be necessary.

TASK

Set the path

before

Oops!

If you type the wrong path, either follow this same procedure to set the path again or reboot your system so that the path statement in the AUTOEXEC.BAT file kicks in.

1. Type **PATH**.

   PATH is the command that you use to tell DOS which directories it should search to find programs. If a directory is listed in the PATH, you don't have to change to that directory to use a command or start a program.

2. Press the **space bar once**.

   Pressing the space bar once inserts a space between the command and the path statement.

3. Type **C:\DOS**.

   DOS is the directory that contains all the DOS program files. Your DOS directory might be named differently. If so, type that directory name.

4. Press **Enter**.

   Pressing Enter confirms the path.

5. Type **PATH** and press **Enter**.

   This step displays the new path. Notice that if you set the path this way, the new path overrides the path in the AUTOEXEC.BAT file. When you restart the computer, however, the AUTOEXEC.BAT file overrides the path.

after

C:\>PATH C:\DOS
C:\>PATH
PATH=C:\DOS
C:\>

Include more than one directory

To include more than one directory in the path, separate the directories by a semicolon—for example, **C:\DOS;C:\WORD**. Don't include a space between directory names.

REVIEW

To set the path

1. Type PATH.
2. Press the space bar once.
3. Type the name of the directory you want to include in the path. Separate each directory name with a semicolon.
4. Press Enter.

Directory does not exist?

If you see the message `Directory does not exist`, a nonexistent directory is contained in the path. When you type a command, DOS tries to search in the nonexistent directory.

TASK

Check memory information

before

Oops!

If you don't understand all the information, don't fret. The key piece of information is the total amount of all memory. If you are a beginner, you don't need to worry about the different types of memory.

1. Type **MEM**.

   MEM is the command to check memory information.

2. Press **Enter**.

   This step executes the command. On-screen you see the total amount of memory your computer contains, the amount that is used, and the amount that is free.

   Different types of memory are reported: conventional, upper, adapter RAM/ROM, extended, and expanded. This information might come in handy if you are calling for support or if a program requires a certain amount of memory.

after

```
C:\>MEM

Memory Type        Total =  Used  +  Free
----------------  -------  ------  ------
Conventional        640K     94K    546K
Upper               187K     68K    119K
Adapter RAM/ROM     197K    197K      0K
Extended (XMS)     7168K   2440K   4728K
Expanded (EMS)        0K      0K      0K
----------------  -------  ------  ------
Total memory       8192K   2799K   5393K

Total under 1 MB    827K    162K    665K

Largest executable program size        546K   (559392 bytes)
Largest free upper memory block         92K    (93856 bytes)
MS-DOS is resident in the high memory area.

C:\>
```

Need complete memory information

For complete information on all types of memory and their uses, see *Using MS-DOS 6,* Special Edition.

REVIEW

To check memory information

1. Type **MEM**.
2. Press **Enter**.

TASK

Optimize memory

before

Oops!

To exit the optimization program, press the F3 key for step 2 or 3 of the Task section.

1. Type **MEMMAKER**.

   This command is used to optimize the memory on your system. DOS will check your hardware, make changes to how the system is set up, and restart your computer twice. The optimization is automatic. You don't really need to know what the changes are; you need to know only that the changes should speed up your computer use.

   A description of how MEMMAKER works appears on-screen. You then have the option to continue or exit.

2. Press **Enter**.

   This step displays the next screen, which tells you the two methods of optimizing memory: Express and Custom. If you are an experienced user, you can use the Custom option. See *Using MS-DOS 6,* Special Edition, for complete information. For most purposes, the Express option—the default—will do.

3. Press **Enter**.

   This step selects the Express option. DOS checks your hard drive and then displays a message telling you that the computer will be restarted.

after

4. Press **Enter**.

   The computer restarts. DOS checks the memory settings and determines the best settings. A message appears stating that the computer will be restarted again so that the new settings will be in effect.

5. Press **Enter**.

   The computer restarts. You see a message that asks whether your system is working properly.

6. Press **Enter**.

   This step tells DOS that the startup was okay. You see a message that the optimization is finished. A table shows the changes that were made.

7. Press **Enter**.

   This step exits the optimization program. You return to the DOS prompt.

Restore original setup

This program makes changes to your AUTOEXEC.BAT and CONFIG.SYS files and saves copies of the original files. The files are named AUTOEXEC.UMB and CONFIG.UMB. If your computer does not work as expected, copy the UMB files over the BAT and SYS files in order to return to the original setup.

Version 6 only

This program is available only with Version 6 of DOS.

REVIEW

1. Type **MEMMAKER**.
2. Press **Enter**.
3. Press **Enter** each time you are prompted.

To optimize memory

Defragment a disk

before

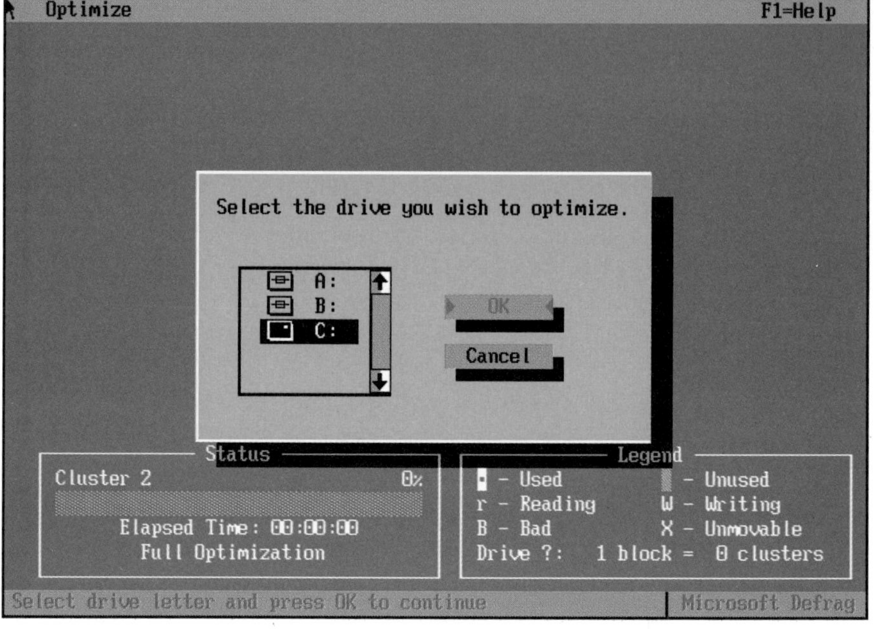

Oops!

To cancel the optimization, select Cancel for step 3. Or press the Esc key and type **x** for step 4.

1. Back up your hard disk.

   Be sure to back up your entire hard disk before you run this program.

2. Type **DEFRAG**.

   This command starts the defragmenter program. Before you run this program, you may want to back up your hard drive.

3. Press **Enter**.

   This step starts the defragmenter program. You are prompted to select the drive to optimize. By default, drive C is selected. The Before screen shows this step.

4. Press **Enter**.

   This step selects drive C. DOS analyzes the hard disk and displays a recommendation. The Optimize button is selected.

   (If the drive doesn't need to be optimized, you'll see a note that says so. Press Enter.)

5. Press **Enter**.

   This step executes the Optimize option. You see the progress of the optimization on-screen. DOS reads the disk and optimizes the files and directories. When it is complete, you see a message that reads `Finished condensing`.

after

6. Press **Enter**.

   This step clears the message and displays a message that reads `Optimization for Drive C Complete.`

7. Press **Tab twice**.

   This step highlights the Exit DEFRAG option.

8. Press **Enter**.

   This step selects the Exit DEFRAG option. You are returned to the DOS prompt.

What is defragmentation?

When DOS saves a file, it sometimes cannot save all the pieces of the file next to each other. Files become fragmented—scattered across the disk. Each time you load a file, DOS has to collect all the respective pieces, and doing so can slow down the computer. Defragmenting the disk puts all the pieces of the files next to each other, which speeds up the computer.

Version 6 only

This program is available only with Version 6 of DOS. Also, you may be unable to use this program when you also use DBLSPACE—another Version 6 program.

REVIEW

To defragment a disk

1. Back up your entire hard drive.
2. Type **DEFRAG**.
3. Press **Enter**.
4. Select the drive you want to optimize and press **Enter**.
5. Press **Enter twice**.
6. Press **Tab twice** to select the Exit DEFRAG option.
7. Press **Enter**.

Using the DOS Shell

This section includes the following commands:

Start the DOS Shell
Make a menu selection
Exit the DOS Shell
Get help
Display files in another directory
Expand directories
Collapse directories
Expand all directories
Select a drive
Display selected files
Sort files
Select a file
Select multiple files
Select all files
Copy a file
Rename a file
Move a file
Delete a file
View file contents
Search for a file
Create a directory
Remove a directory

TASK

Start the DOS Shell

before

Oops!

To exit the DOS Shell, see *TASK: Exit the DOS Shell*.

1. At the DOS prompt, type **DOSSHELL**.

   DOSSHELL is the command to start the DOS Shell program.

   Your computer may be set up to start the DOS Shell automatically. In this case, you don't need to follow this exercise. You will see the DOS Shell screen every time you start your computer.

2. Press **Enter**.

   Pressing Enter confirms the command. You see a message as DOS reads the disk information and counts the files and directories. Then you see the DOS Shell screen.

   The first line of the screen lists the program name—`MS-DOS Shell`. Below the title you see the menu bar. The DOS Shell has its own menu system. Menus include File, Options, View, Tree, and Help.

   Below the menu bar, you see the name of the current directory—in this case, the root or main directory.

   The next part of the screen shows the drive icons. An *icon* is a pictorial representation of each drive on your computer.

after

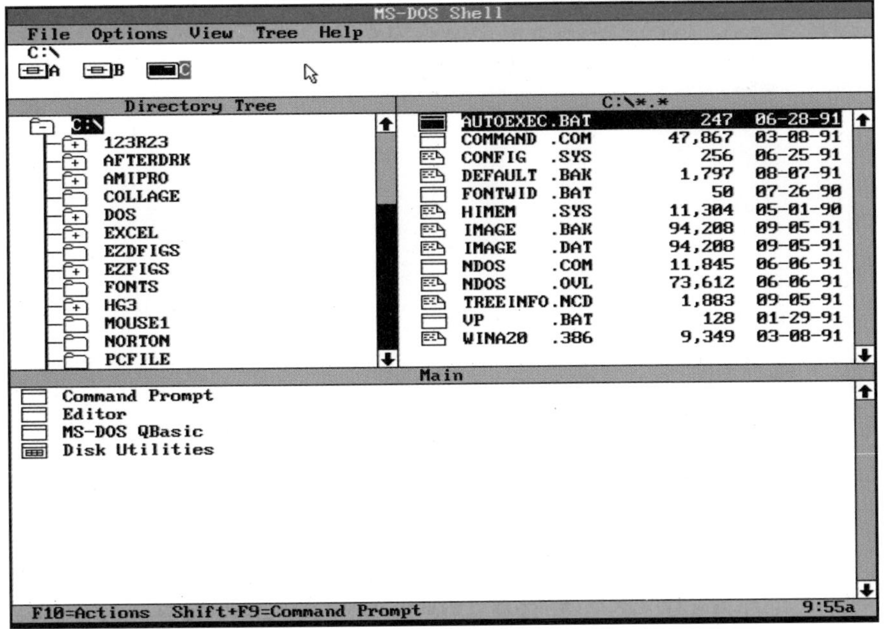

On the left side of the middle of the screen, you see the Directory Tree window. This window contains icons that look like folders. Each folder represents a directory. These are called *directory icons*. The directories are listed in alphabetical order. Note that some directory icons have a + (plus sign) on them. This symbol indicates that these directories contain other directories. You can expand and collapse the directories shown. (See other tasks in this section for more information.)

The right side of the middle of the screen, called the *file list*, lists the files in the current directory.

The bottom of the screen is called the *program list*. You use this area to start DOS applications and utilities. See *Using MS-DOS 6*, Special Edition, for complete information on using the program list.

Move around the screen

You can move around four areas of the screen: the drive icon area, the Directory Tree window, the file list, and the program list. Press the Tab key to move forward from area to area. Press the Shift-Tab key combination to move backward.

Main doesn't appear?

If `Main` doesn't appear at the bottom of the screen, press the Alt-V key combination. Then select Program/File Lists. The view might be set to single file list.

REVIEW

To start the DOS Shell

1. At the DOS prompt, type **DOSSHELL**.
2. Press **Enter**.

TASK

Make a menu selection

before

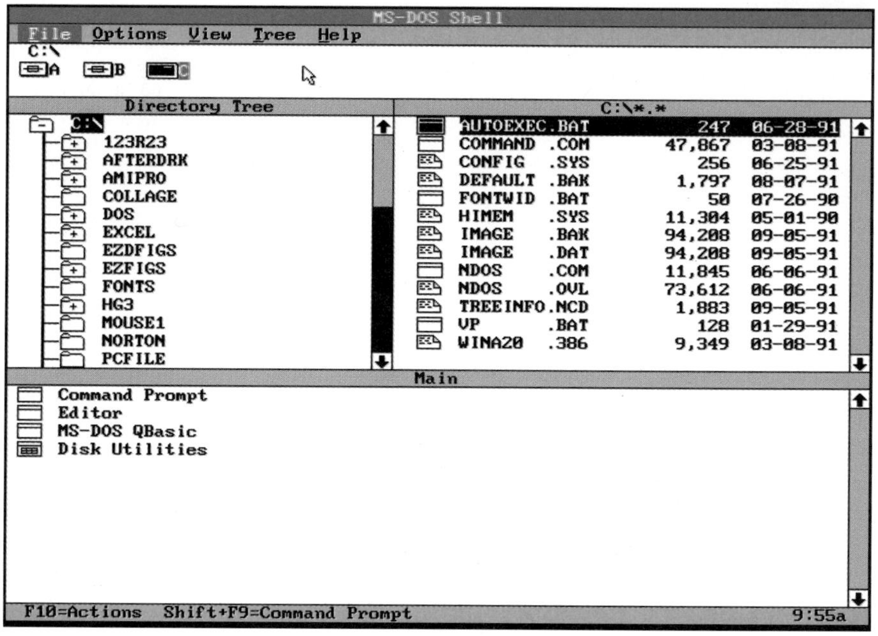

MS-DOS Shell			

File Options View Tree Help
C:\

A B C

Directory Tree: C:\, 123R23, AFTERDRK, AMIPRO, COLLAGE, DOS, EXCEL, EZDFIGS, EZFIGS, FONTS, HG3, MOUSE1, NORTON, PCFILE

C:*.*

File	Ext	Size	Date
AUTOEXEC	.BAT	247	06-28-91
COMMAND	.COM	47,867	03-08-91
CONFIG	.SYS	256	06-25-91
DEFAULT	.BAK	1,797	08-07-91
FONTWID	.BAT	50	07-26-90
HIMEM	.SYS	11,304	05-01-90
IMAGE	.BAK	94,208	09-05-91
IMAGE	.DAT	94,208	09-05-91
NDOS	.COM	11,845	06-06-91
NDOS	.OVL	73,612	06-06-91
TREEINFO	.NCD	1,883	09-05-91
VP	.BAT	128	01-29-91
WINA20	.386	9,349	03-08-91

Main: Command Prompt, Editor, MS-DOS QBasic, Disk Utilities

F10=Actions Shift+F9=Command Prompt 9:55a

Oops!

To close a menu without making a selection, press the Esc key.

1. Press Alt.

Pressing the Alt key activates the menu bar. The first menu, File, is selected.

2. Type F.

Typing F opens the File menu. You see a list of File commands.

To select the menu to open, you can either press the Alt key and type the underlined letter in the menu name, or you can press Alt and use the arrow keys to move to the menu name and then press Enter.

3. Type x.

Typing x selects the Exit command. The command is executed. In this case, you return to the DOS prompt. For other commands, you might see a dialog box that prompts you for additional information.

To select a command, you can either type the underlined letter in the command name, or you can use the arrow keys to move to the command name and then press Enter.

after

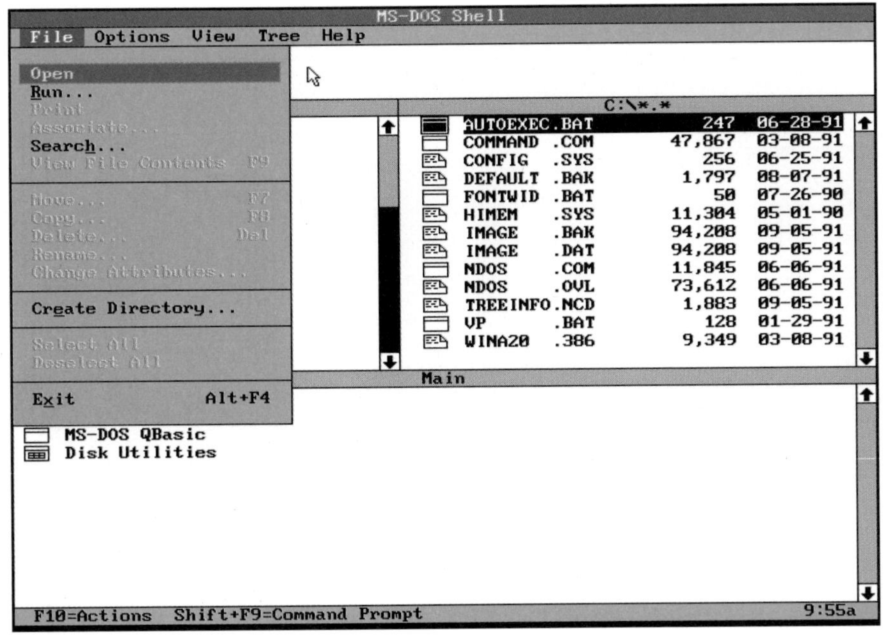

Command dimmed?

If a command is dimmed or missing, that command is not available for the current window. If the cursor is in the Directory Tree window, for example, the Copy command is not available because you cannot copy directories.

REVIEW

To make a menu selection

1. Press **Alt**.
2. Type the underlined letter of the menu name or use the arrow keys to move to the menu name and then press **Enter**.
3. Type the underlined letter of the command name. You also can use the arrow keys to move to the command name and then press **Enter**.

Use the mouse

To make a menu selection by using the mouse, click on the menu name. Then click on the command name.

TASK

Exit the DOS Shell

before

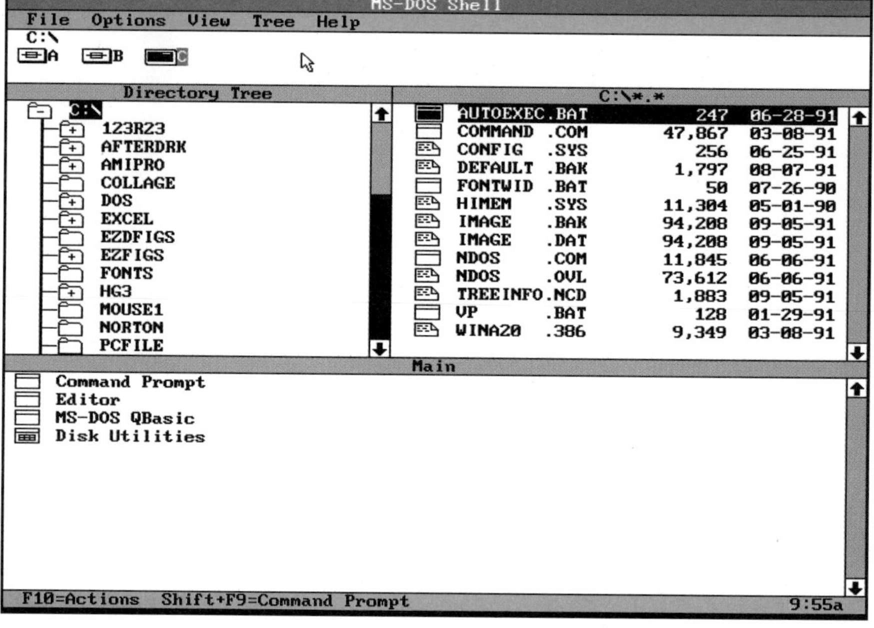

Oops!

To restart the DOS Shell, type **DOSSHELL** at the DOS prompt.

1. Press **Alt**.

   Pressing the Alt key activates the menu bar. The first menu, File, is highlighted.

2. Type **F**.

   Typing F opens the File menu. You see a list of File commands.

3. Type **x**.

   Typing x selects the Exit command. You return to the DOS prompt.

after

Try a shortcut

Press the Alt-F4 key combination or the F3 key to select the File Exit command.

REVIEW

To exit the DOS SHELL

1. Press **Alt**.
2. Type **F** to open the File menu.
3. Type **x** to select the Exit command.

TASK

Get help

before

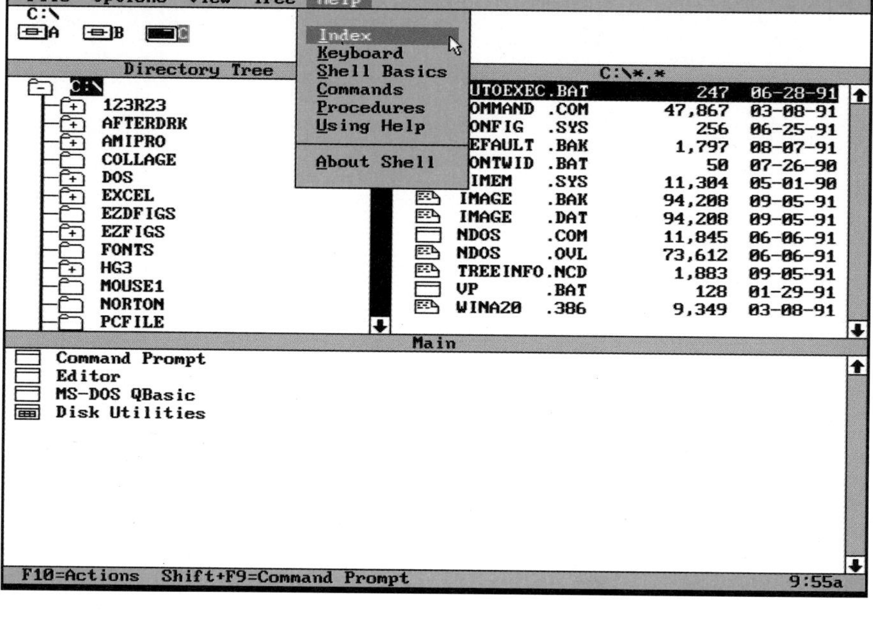

Oops!

To close the Help window, press the Esc key.

1. Start the DOS Shell.

   For help with this step, see *TASK: Start the DOS Shell*. If the DOS Shell is already started, skip this step.

2. Press **Alt**.

   Pressing the Alt key activates the menu bar.

3. Type **H**.

   Typing H opens the Help menu. You see a list of Help commands.

4. Type **I**.

   Typing I selects the Index command. You see an explanation of how to select a topic and an index of topics.

5. Press **Tab** until you highlight **Movement Keys**.

   This step selects the Movement Keys topic. Pressing the Shift-Tab key combination moves the cursor backward through the list. You may not be able to see the selected topic within the window. To scroll through the window, press ↑ or ↓. The selected topic is boxed. (On color monitors, it also appears in a different color.)

after

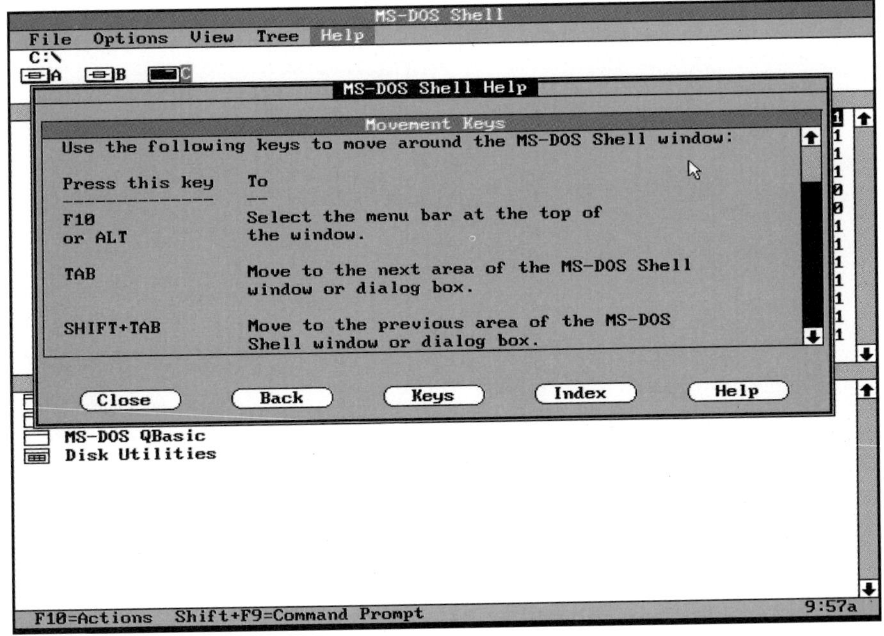

6. Press **Enter**.

   Pressing Enter displays help about the selected topic—in this case, about movement keys.

7. Press **Esc**.

   Pressing the Esc key closes the Help window.

Use other options

You can use other Help options. For more information, see *Using MS-DOS 6*, Special Edition.

REVIEW

To get help

1. Start the DOS Shell.
2. Press **Alt** to activate the menu bar.
3. Type **H** to open the Help menu.
4. Type **I** to select the Index command.
5. Press **Tab** until you highlight the command you want.
6. Press **Enter** to display Help.
7. Press **Esc** to close the Help window.

TASK

Display files in another directory

before

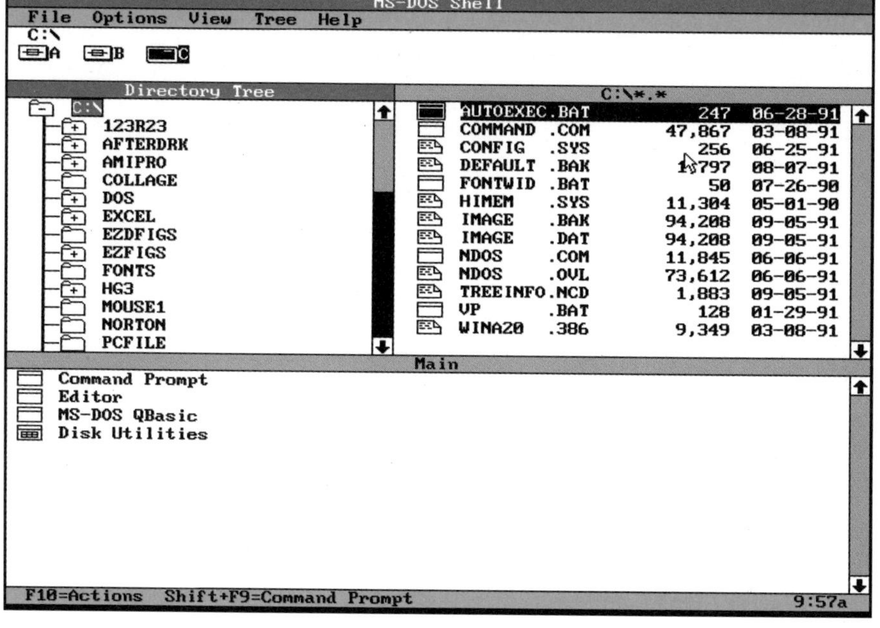

1. Start the DOS Shell.

   For help with this step, see *TASK: Start the DOS Shell*. If the DOS Shell is already started, skip this step.

2. Press **Tab** until the Directory Tree window is highlighted.

   This step moves you to the Directory Tree window.

3. Press ↓ until the DOS directory is highlighted.

   Pressing ↓ moves you through the list of directories. As a new directory is highlighted, the files in that directory appear in the file list. When you move to the DOS directory, for example, you see in the right window the files in that directory.

Oops!

Be sure to press Tab to move to the Directory Tree window. Pressing ↓ in the drive icon window does nothing; pressing ↓ in the file list selects a file.

after

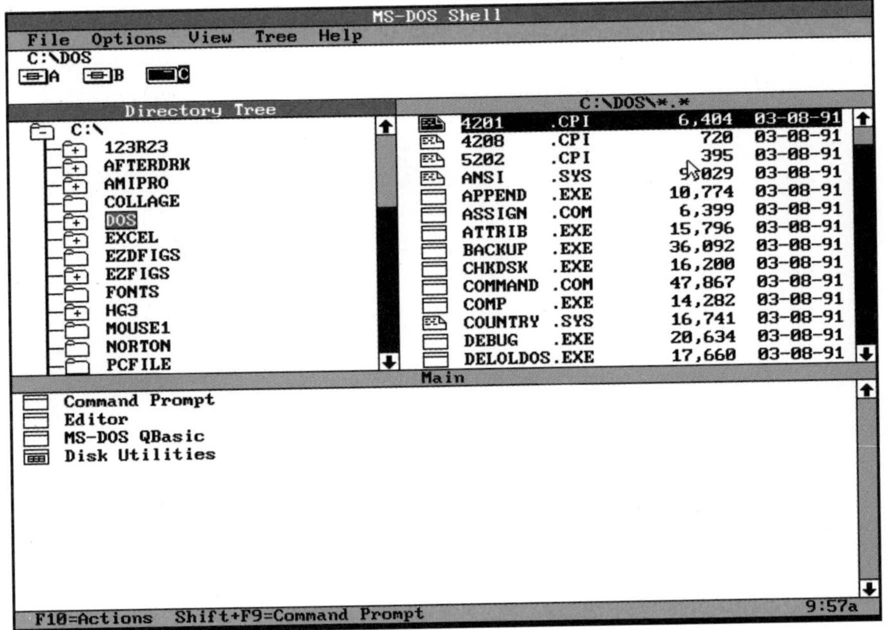

Expand list

To see other directories, expand the directory listing. See *TASK: Expand directories* and *TASK: Expand all directories.*

REVIEW

To display files in another directory

1. Start the DOS Shell.
2. Press **Tab** to move to the Directory Tree window.
3. Press ↓ or ↑ to highlight the directory you want.

Use the mouse

To select a directory by using the mouse, click on the directory name.

Expand directories

before

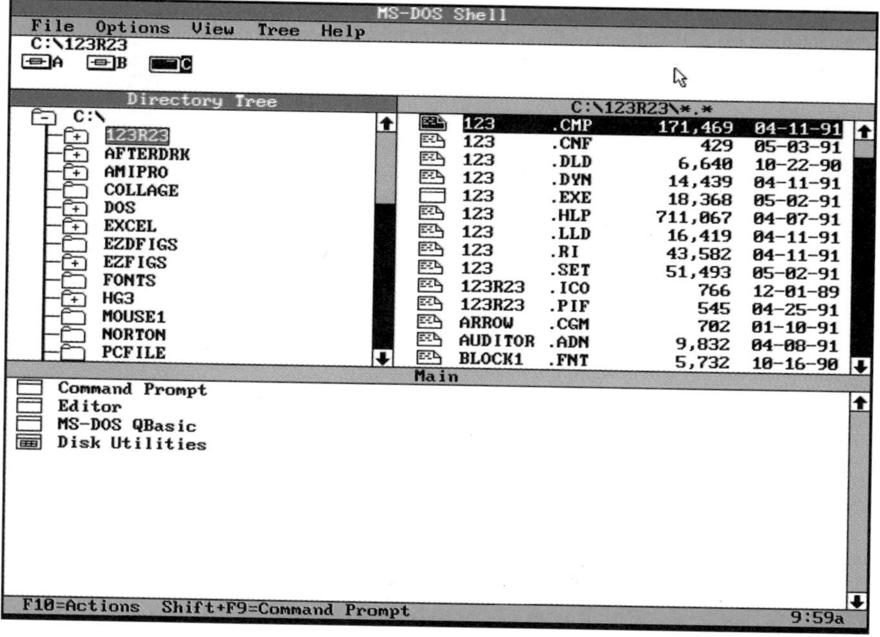

1. **Start the DOS Shell.**

   For help with this step, see *TASK: Start the DOS Shell*. If the DOS Shell is already started, skip this step.

2. **Press Tab until you move to the Directory Tree window.**

   This step moves you to the Directory Tree window. This window lists the current directories.

3. **Press ↓ or ↑ until you highlight a directory with an icon that contains a plus sign (+).**

   In the example, the directory 123R23 is highlighted. If you don't have this directory, highlight one you do have. Make sure that its icon is marked with a plus sign (+). A plus sign indicates that a directory contains other directories. The Before screen shows this step.

4. **Press Alt.**

   Pressing the Alt key activates the menu bar.

5. **Type T.**

   Typing T opens the Tree menu. You see a list of commands.

Oops!

If the command is dimmed, that command is not available for the selected directory. The directory probably does not contain other directories. Be sure that the directory icon has a plus sign on it before you try to expand it.

after

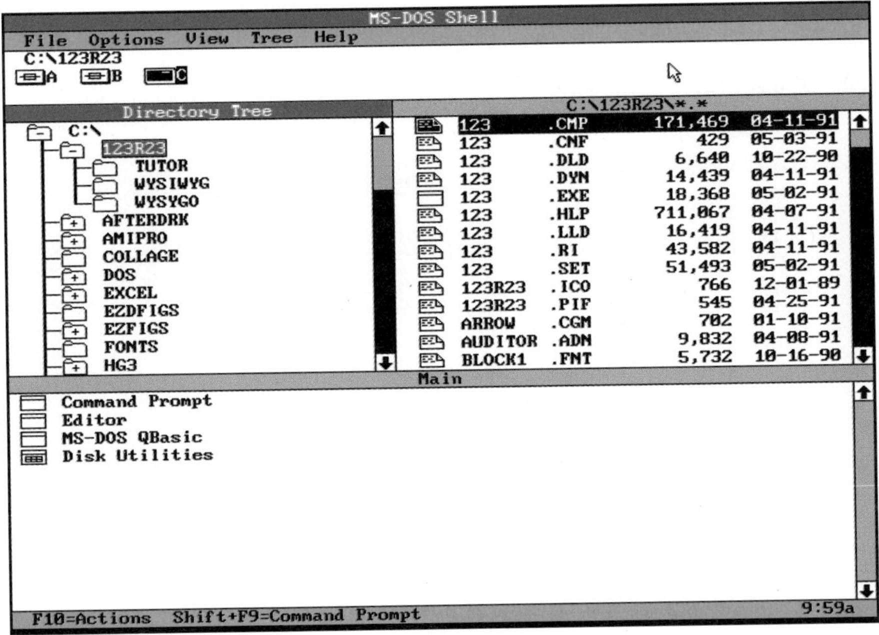

6. Type **B**.

Typing B selects the Expand Branch command. All levels of directories within the selected directory (123R23) appear. If these directories contain other directories, you also see these other directories.

Note that the directory icon is now marked with a minus sign (–). This sign reminds you that you can collapse the directory if you want. See *TASK: Collapse directories* for more information.

Expand just one level

To expand just one level, use the Expand One Level command from the Tree menu.

REVIEW

To expand directories

1. Start the DOS Shell.
2. Press **Tab** to move to the Directory Tree window.
3. Press ↓ or ↑ to highlight the directory you want to expand. Make sure that the icon contains a plus sign (+).
4. Press **Alt** to activate the menu bar.
5. Type **T** to open the Tree menu.
6. Type **B** to select Expand Branch.

Try a shortcut

Highlight the directory and then press * (asterisk) or + (plus) to expand the directory.

Collapse directories

before

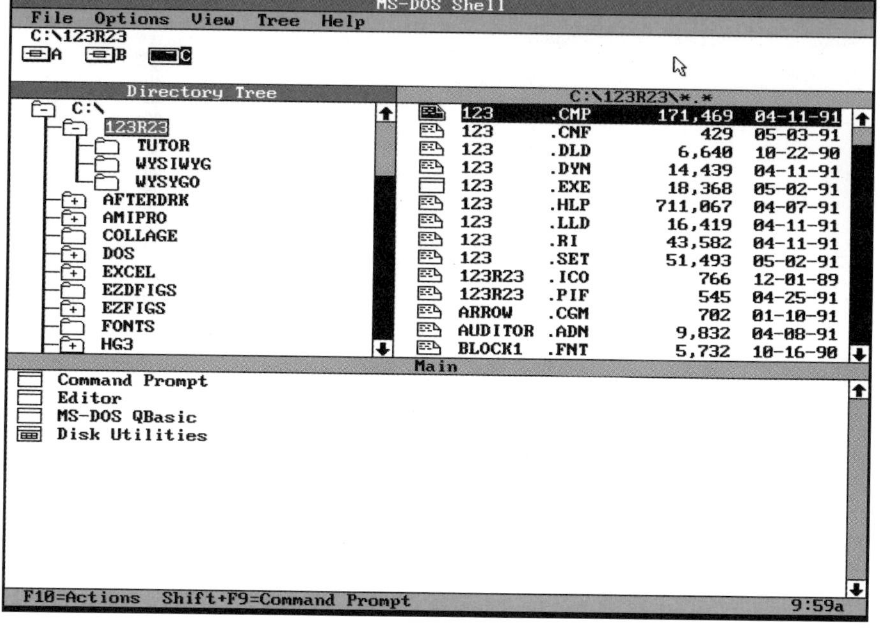

Oops!

To expand a directory, see *TASK: Expand directories.*

1. Start the DOS Shell.

   For help with this step, see *TASK: Start the DOS Shell*. If the DOS Shell is already started, skip this step.

2. Press **Tab** until you move to the Directory Tree window.

   This step moves you to the Directory Tree window. This window lists the current directories.

3. Press ↓ or ↑ until you highlight a directory with an icon that contains a minus sign (–).

   Remember that you first have to expand a directory before you can collapse it. If the directory contains a plus sign (+), expand it first. (See *TASK: Expand directories*.)

   In the example, the directory 123R23 is highlighted. If you don't have this directory, highlight one you do have. Make sure that its icon contains a minus sign. The Before screen shows this step.

4. Press **Alt**.

   Pressing the Alt key activates the menu bar.

5. Type **T**.

   Typing T opens the Tree menu. You see a list of commands.

after

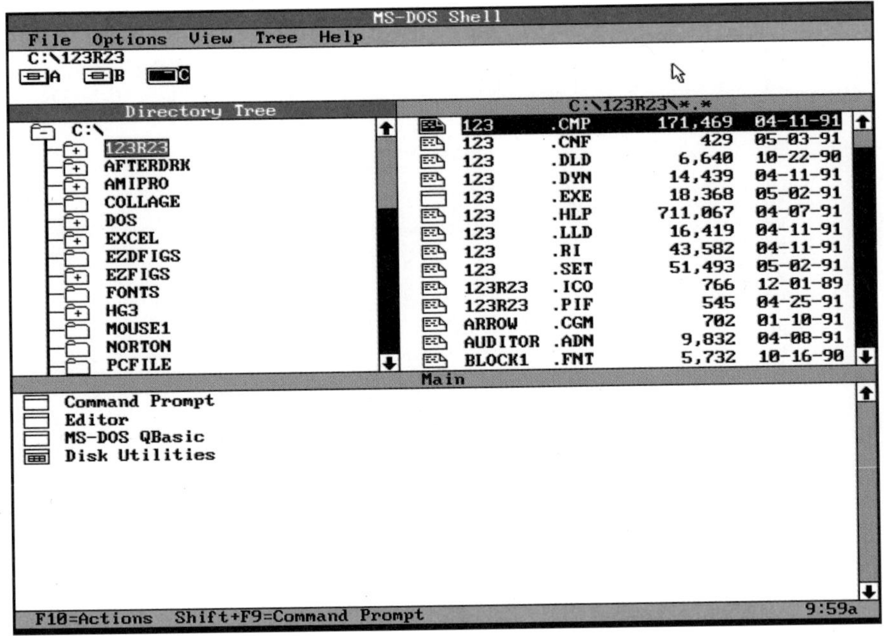

Use the Expand One Level command

If the root directory is selected and you select Collapse Branch, you see `C:\` in the Directory Tree window. Use the Expand One Level command to expand the directory list to the original list.

6. Type **C**.

   Typing C selects the Collapse Branch command and collapses the directory. Only the parent directory appears (the directory that contains the other directories).

REVIEW

To collapse directories

1. Start the DOS Shell.
2. Press **Tab** to move to the Directory Tree window.
3. Press ↑ or ↓ to highlight the directory you want to collapse. Be sure that the directory contains a minus sign (–).
4. Press **Alt** to activate the menu bar.
5. Type **T** to open the Tree menu.
6. Type **C** to select Collapse Branch.

Try a shortcut

Highlight the directory and then press – (minus) to collapse the directory.

TASK

Expand all directories

before

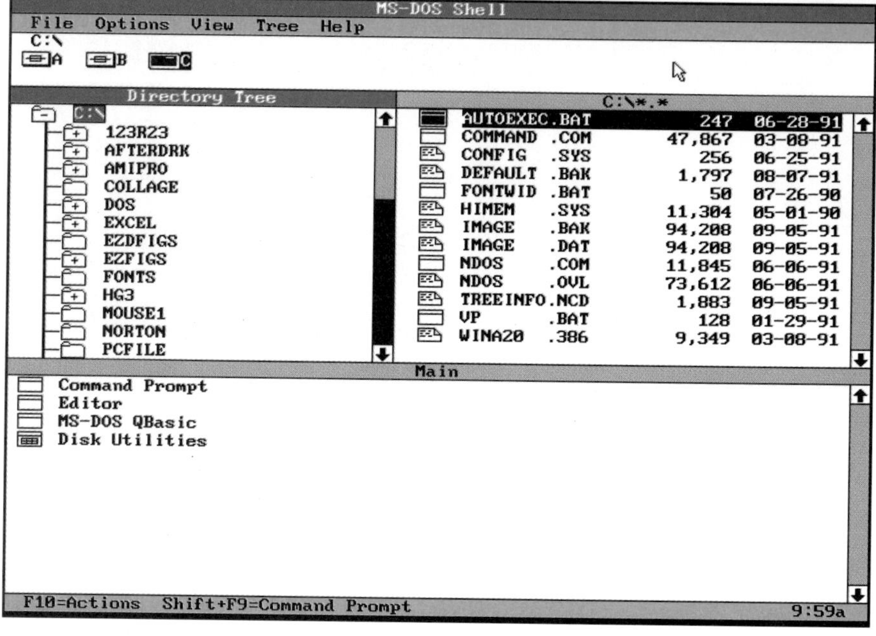

1. **Start the DOS Shell.**

   For help with this step, see *TASK: Start the DOS Shell*. If the DOS Shell is already started, skip this step.

2. **Press Tab until you move to the Directory Tree window.**

   This step moves you to the Directory Tree window. This window lists the current directories.

3. **Make sure that the root directory is highlighted.**

   The root directory should be highlighted when you press Tab. If it is not highlighted, use ↑ or ↓ to select this directory. Remember that the root directory is named \ (backslash). For instance, C:\ indicates that the root directory is on drive C.

4. **Press Alt.**

   Pressing the Alt key activates the menu bar.

5. **Type T.**

   Typing T opens the Tree menu. You see a list of commands.

6. **Type A.**

   Typing A selects the Expand All command. All the directories appear.

   You can collapse selected branches of the directory. See *TASK: Collapse directories* for more information.

Oops!

To collapse all the directories (you will see C:\ on-screen), highlight the root directory, and then press the Alt key, type T, and then type C.

after

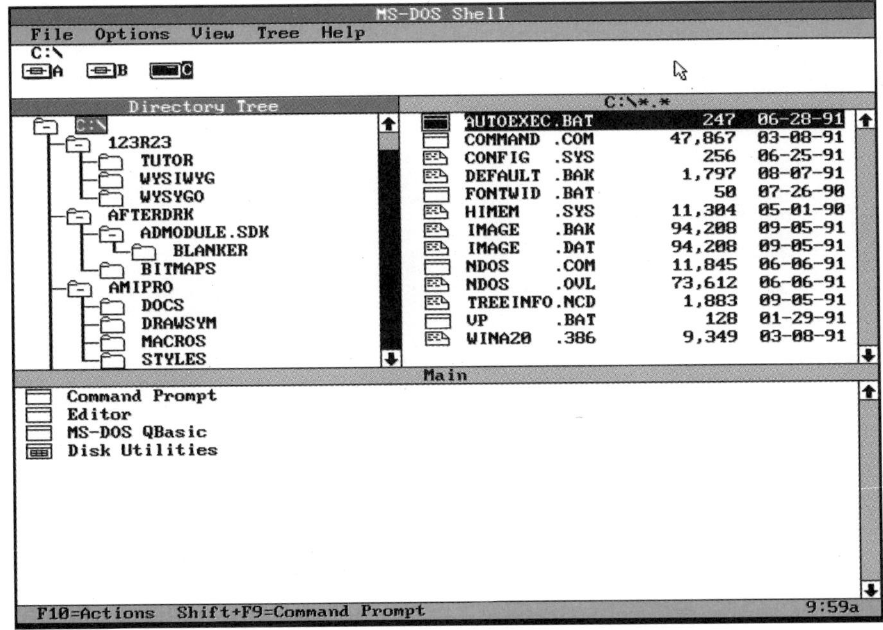

REVIEW

To expand all directories

1. Start the DOS Shell.
2. Press **Tab** to move to the Directory Tree window.
3. Make sure that the root directory is highlighted.
4. Press **Alt** to activate the menu bar.
5. Type **T** to open the Tree menu.
6. Type **A** to select Expand All.

TASK

Select a drive

before

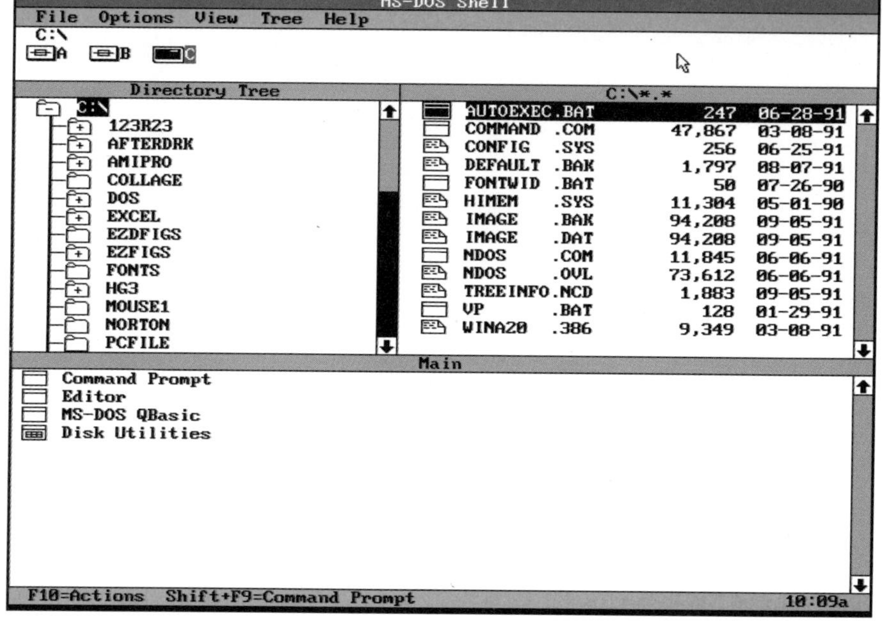

Oops!

If you get a warning message, make sure that the disk is inserted and the drive door is closed. Then press Enter to select the option named `Try to read this disk again.`

1. Start the DOS Shell.

   For help with this step, see *TASK: Start the DOS Shell*. If the DOS Shell is already started, skip this step.

2. Insert a disk into floppy drive A.

   Every computer has at least one floppy drive, called drive A. You also might have other floppy drives. Insert a disk into drive A in your computer. Be sure to close the drive door.

3. Press **Tab** until you move to the drive icon area.

   This step moves you to the drive icon area. The drive icon area is just beneath the menu bar. The cursor may already be in this area.

4. Press → or ← until you highlight the drive A icon.

   Pressing → or ← selects drive A. (The current position of the cursor will determine whether you need to press → to move right or ← to move left.) The drive letter is highlighted.

5. Press **Enter**.

   Pressing Enter displays the directories on this drive in the Directory Tree window and the files in the file list window.

after

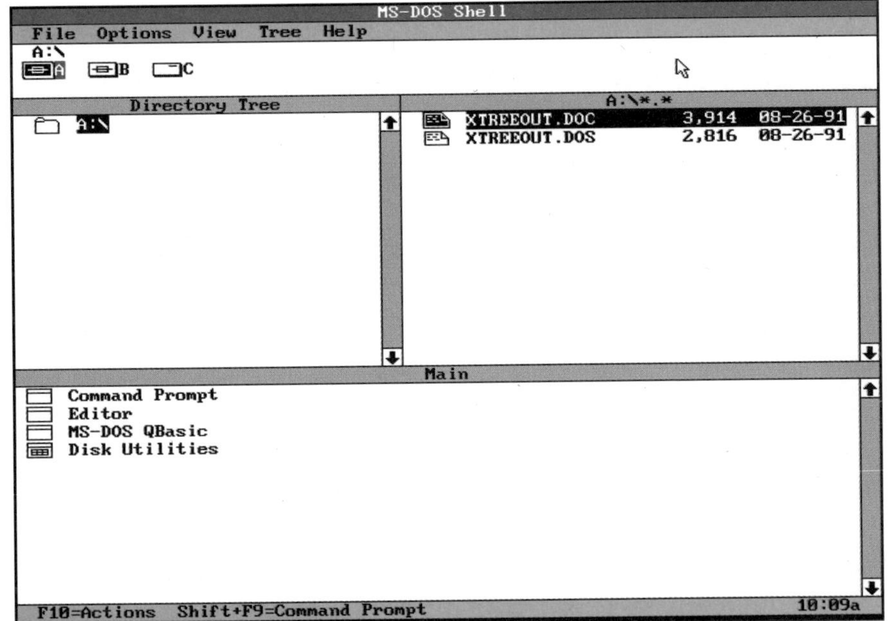

Return to drive C

To move back to drive C, press → to highlight drive C; then press Enter.

REVIEW

To select a drive

1. Start the DOS Shell.
2. Insert a disk into the drive.
3. Press **Tab** to move to the drive icon area.
4. Press → or ← to highlight the drive.
5. Press **Enter**.

Use the correct keys

↑ and ↓ do not work in the drive icon window. You must press → and ←.

Display selected files

before

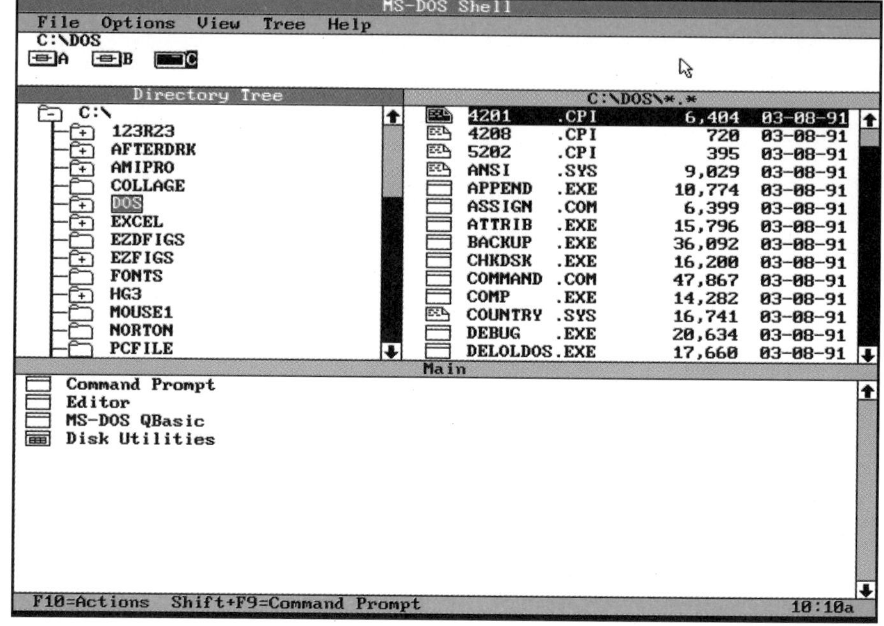

Oops!

To view all files again, follow this same procedure, but type ***.*** instead of typing ***.SYS**.

1. Start the DOS Shell.

For help with this step, see *TASK: Start the DOS Shell*. If the DOS Shell is already started, skip this step.

2. Press **Tab** until you move to the Directory Tree window.

This step moves the cursor to the Directory Tree window.

3. Press ↑ or ↓ until the DOS directory is highlighted.

Pressing ↑ or ↓ highlights the directory for which you want to display files. (The current position of the cursor will determine whether you need to press ↑ to move up or ↓ to move down.) If you don't have a directory named DOS, highlight one that you do have.

4. Press **Alt**.

Pressing the Alt key activates the menu bar.

5. Type **O**.

Typing O opens the Options menu. You see a list of Options commands.

6. Type **F**.

Typing F selects the File Display Options command. You see the File Display Options dialog box. Within this box is a Name: text box that displays *.*. This specification (called star-dot-star) tells the DOS Shell to display all files.

after

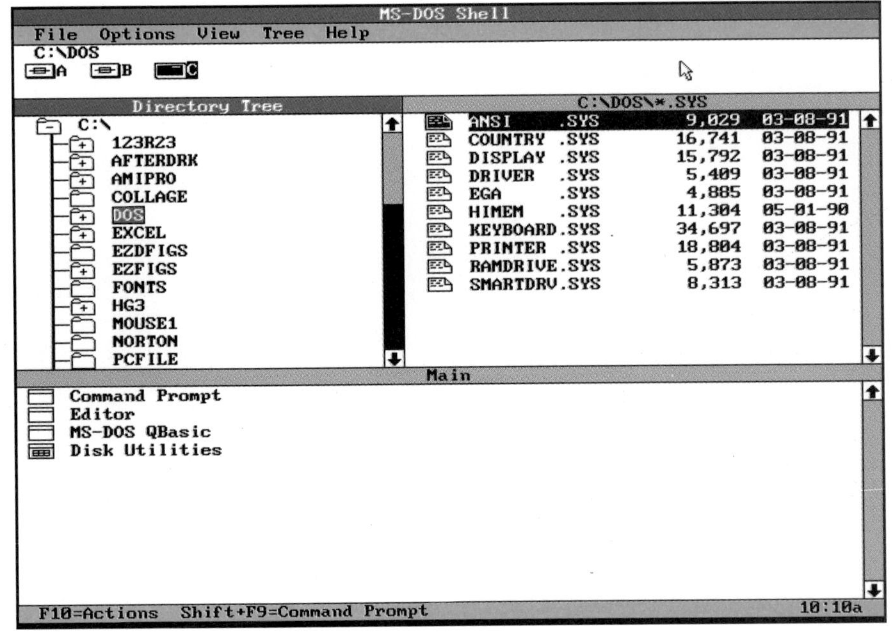

7. Type ***.SYS**.

   This step tells the DOS Shell to display files that have any root name, but that have the SYS extension. (* is a wild card that can represent any characters and any number of characters.)

8. Press **Enter**.

   Pressing Enter confirms the command. You see only the SYS files in the file list window.

What is a wild card?

A wild card is a character that matches any character or characters. The question mark wild card (?) matches a single character. The asterisk wild card (*) matches all characters.

Display other files

Use this same procedure to list other files. For example, in the Name: text box, type **S*.*** to list all files that start with S. Type **FO*.COM** to match all files that start with FO and have the extension COM. Type **ASSIGN.COM** to display the file named ASSIGN.COM.

REVIEW

To display selected files

1. Start the DOS Shell.
2. Press **Tab** to move to the Directory Tree window.
3. Use ↑ or ↓ to highlight the directory for which you want to display selected files.
4. Press **Alt** to activate the menu bar.
5. Type **O** to open the Options menu.
6. Type **F** to select the File Display Options command.
7. In the Name text box, type the file name you want to display. Use wild cards if you want.
8. Press **Enter**.

Sort files

before

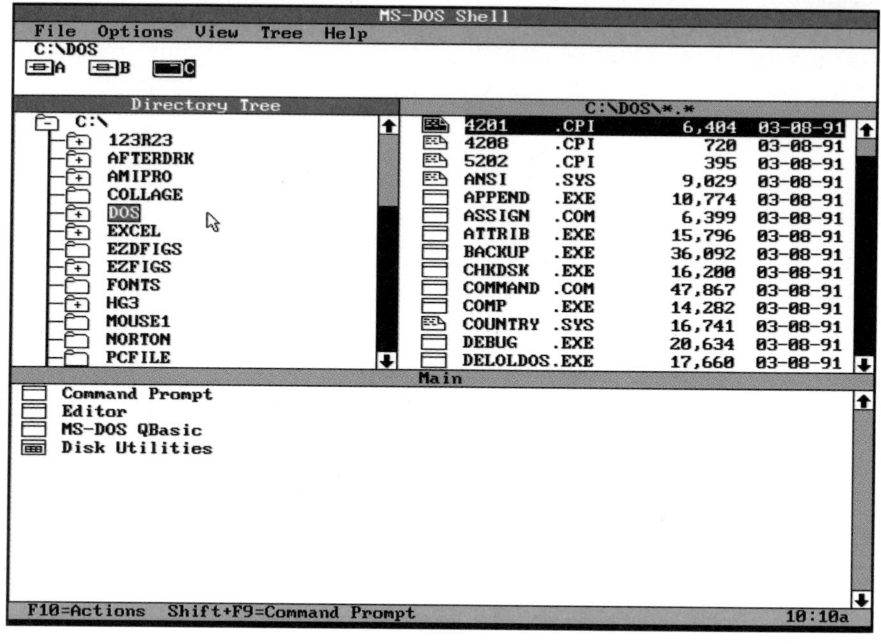

Oops!

To sort files by name, follow this same procedure, but select Name rather than Extension.

1. **Start the DOS Shell.**

   For help with this step, see *TASK: Start the DOS Shell.*

2. **Press Tab until you move to the Directory Tree window.**

   This step moves the cursor to the Directory Tree window.

3. **Press ↑ or ↓ until the DOS directory is highlighted.**

   Pressing ↑ or ↓ highlights the directory for which you want to display and sort files.

4. **Press Alt.**

   Pressing the Alt key activates the menu bar.

5. **Type O.**

   This step opens the Options menu.

6. **Type F.**

   This step selects the File Display Options command. You see the File Display Options dialog box. Within this box is a text box that displays *.*. (See *TASK: Display certain files.*) This box also lists Sort by options, which enable you to specify how items are sorted.

7. **Press Tab three times.**

   This step moves the cursor to the Sort by options.

after

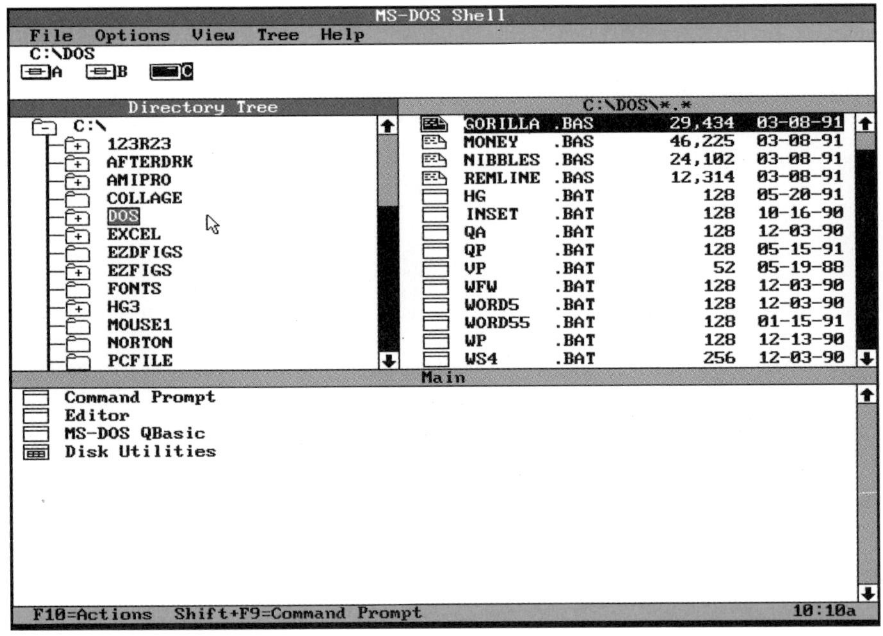

8. Press ↓.

   Pressing ↓ selects the Extension option. You can tell this option is selected because the button next to the sort name is filled in. This option tells the DOS Shell to sort the files in the directory by extension. (The default list is sorted by name.)

9. Press **Enter**.

   Pressing Enter confirms the command.

Use other sort options

You also can sort by date, size, and other options. See *Using MS-DOS 6*, Special Edition, for complete information on sort options.

REVIEW

To sort files

1. Start the DOS Shell.
2. Press **Tab** to move to the Directory Tree window.
3. Use ↑ or ↓ to highlight the directory for which you want to sort files.
4. Press **Alt** to activate the menu bar.
5. Type **O** to open the Options menu.
6. Type **F** to select the File Display Options command.
7. Press **Tab** to move to the Sort by options.
8. Press ↓ until the sort option you want is selected.
9. Press **Enter**.

Select a file

before

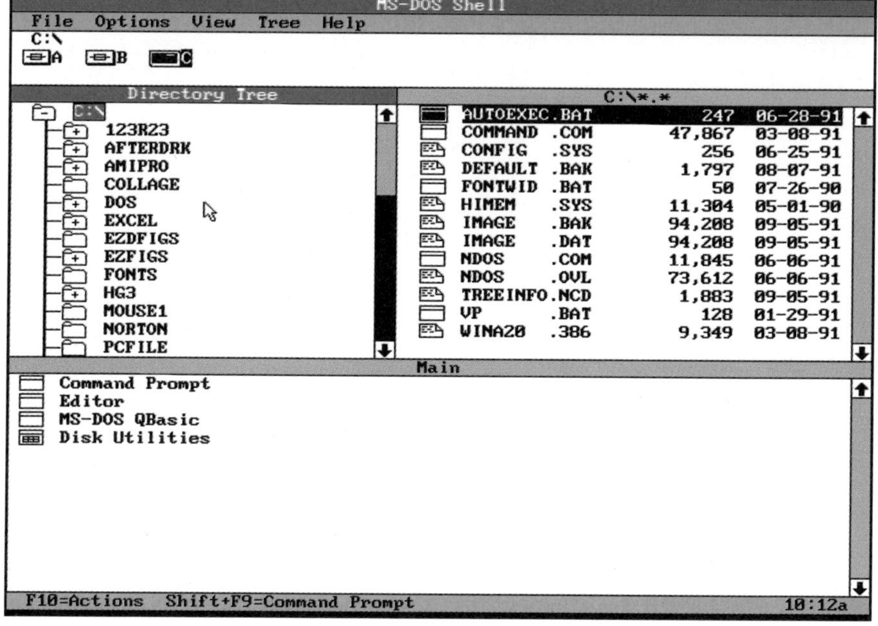

Oops!

If you highlight the wrong file, press ↑ or ↓ to move to the correct file.

1. Start the DOS Shell.

   For help with this step, see *TASK: Start the DOS Shell*. If the DOS Shell is already started, skip this step.

2. Press **Tab** until you move to the Directory Tree window.

   This step moves the cursor to the Directory Tree window. The root directory will probably be selected. If it isn't, press ↑ to highlight the root directory.

3. Press **Tab** to move to the file list.

   This step moves the cursor to the file list. You can tell that the file list is selected because the title bar changes color or intensity.

   To select a file, you must be in the file list window. If you are in the Directory Tree window, you can press ↓ or ↑ to move among the directories.

4. Press ↑ or ↓ to highlight the file CONFIG.SYS.

   This step highlights the file you want to select. If you don't have this file, highlight one you do have. After you select a file, you can perform operations, such as copying it, moving it, deleting it, and so on. See the other tasks in this section.

after

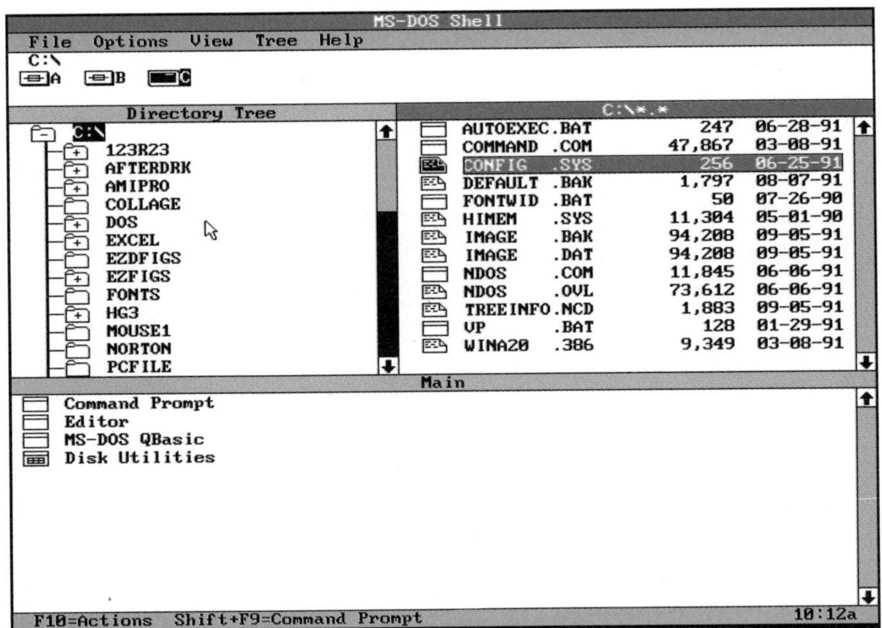

Use the mouse

To select a file by using the mouse, click on the file name.

REVIEW

To select a file

1. Start the DOS Shell.
2. If necessary, press **Tab** to move to the Directory Tree window; then select the directory that contains the file.
3. Press **Tab** to move to the file list window.
4. Use ↑ or ↓ to highlight the file.

Select files in other directories

To select a file in another directory, first highlight the directory in the Directory Tree window. The files for the highlighted directory will appear in the file list window. Press Tab to move to the file list window; then select the file.

Select multiple files

before

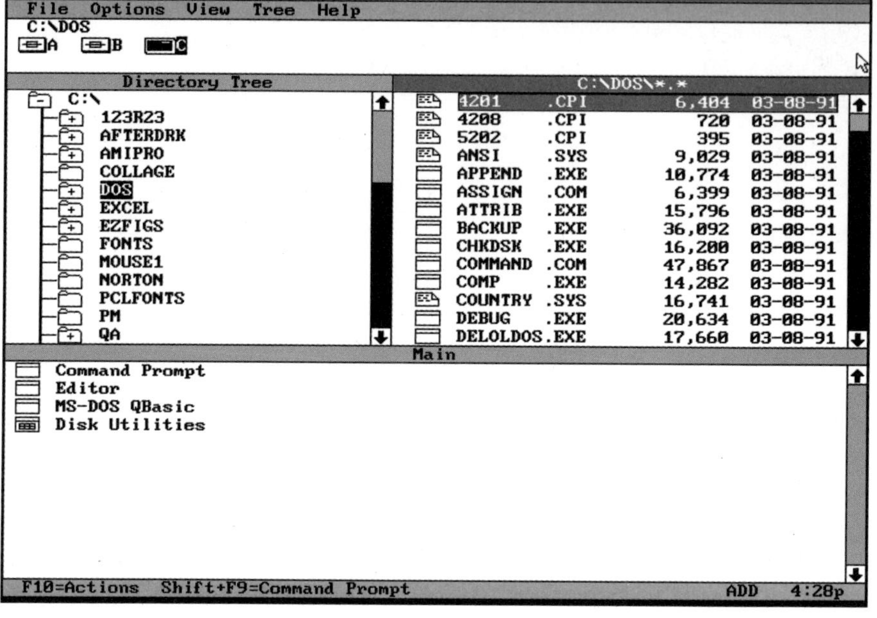

1. Start the DOS Shell.

   For help with this step, see *TASK: Start the DOS Shell*. If the DOS Shell is already started, skip this step.

2. Press **Tab** to move to the Directory Tree window.

   This step moves the cursor to the Directory Tree window so that you can select the directory you want.

3. Press ↑ or ↓ until you highlight the DOS directory.

   This step selects the directory. If you don't have a directory named DOS, select one that you do have.

4. Press **Tab** to move to the file list window.

   This step moves the cursor to the file list window so that you can select the files.

5. Press ↑ or ↓ to move to the file ANSI.SYS.

   This step moves the cursor to the file you want to select. If you don't have a file named ANSI.SYS, select one you do have.

6. Press **Shift-F8**.

   This step turns on Add mode. While in Add mode, you can add Selected files.

Oops!

To deselect a file, move the cursor to the file that you want to deselect and press the space bar again.

after

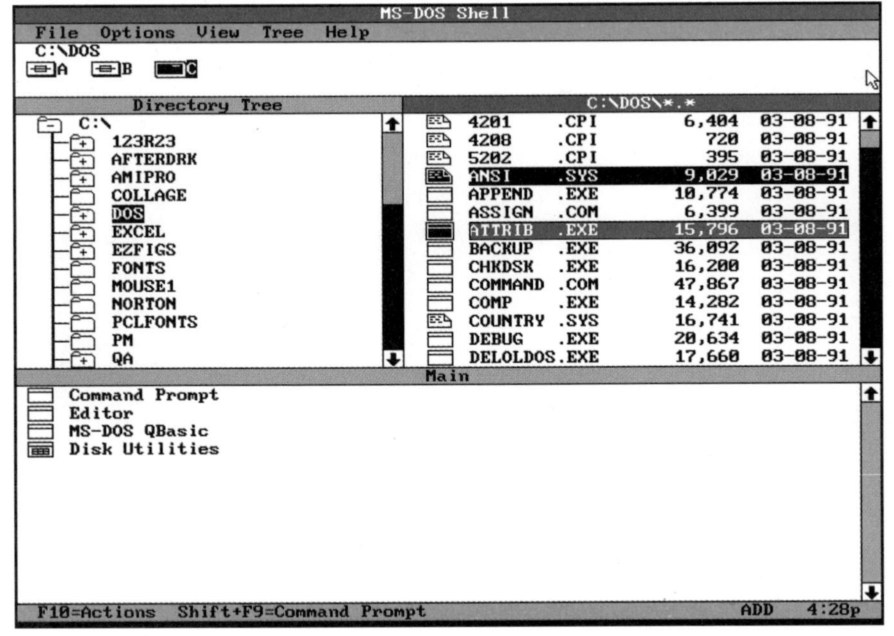

7. Press ↑ or ↓ to move to the file ATTRIB.EXE.

   This step moves the cursor to the next file you want to select.

8. Press **Ctrl-space bar**.

   This step selects the ATTRIB.EXE file; both files are selected.

Select continuous files

To select a continuous list of files, move the cursor to the first file you want to select. Then hold down the Shift key and use the arrow keys to highlight the other files. Release the Shift key when you have selected the files.

REVIEW

To select multiple files

1. Start the DOS Shell.
2. If necessary, press **Tab** to move to the Directory Tree window; then select the directory that contains the files you want to select.
3. Press **Tab** to move to the file list window.
4. Press ↑ or ↓ to move to the file you want to select.
5. Press the **Shift-F8**.
6. Continue moving to files and pressing **Ctrl-space bar** until you select all the files you want.

Turn off Add mode

Press Shift-F8 again to turn off Add mode.

Select all files

before

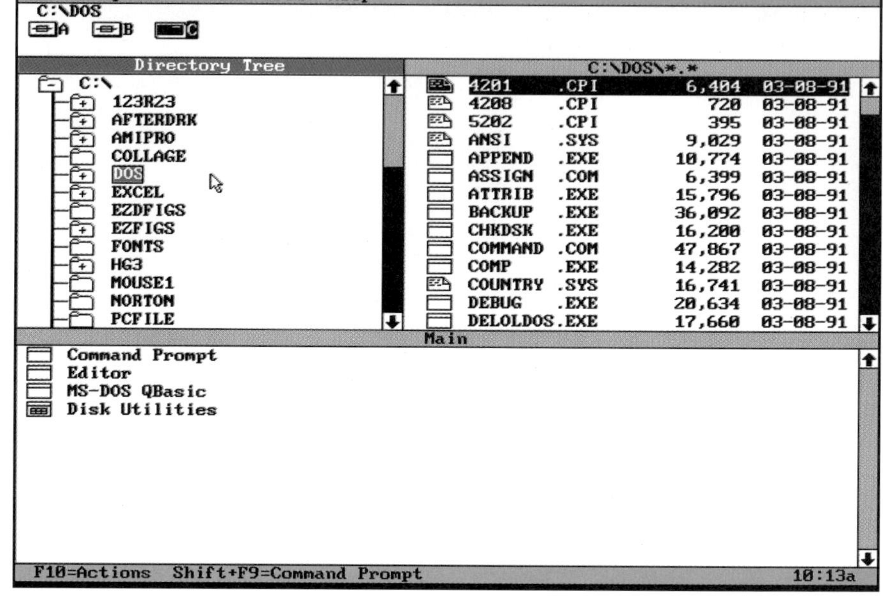

Oops!

To deselect files, press Alt, type F, and then type l (lowercase L) to select the Deselect All command.

1. Start the DOS Shell.

   For help with this step, see *TASK: Start the DOS Shell*. If the DOS Shell is already started, skip this step.

2. Press **Tab** to move to the Directory Tree window.

   This step moves the cursor to the Directory Tree window so that you can first select the directory you want.

3. Press ↑ or ↓ until you highlight the DOS directory.

   This step selects the directory. If you don't have a directory named DOS, select one that you do have.

4. Press **Tab** to move to the file list window.

   This step moves the cursor to the file list window so that you can select the files.

5. Press **Alt**.

   Pressing the Alt key activates the menu bar.

6. Type **F**.

   This step opens the File menu. You see a list of File commands.

after

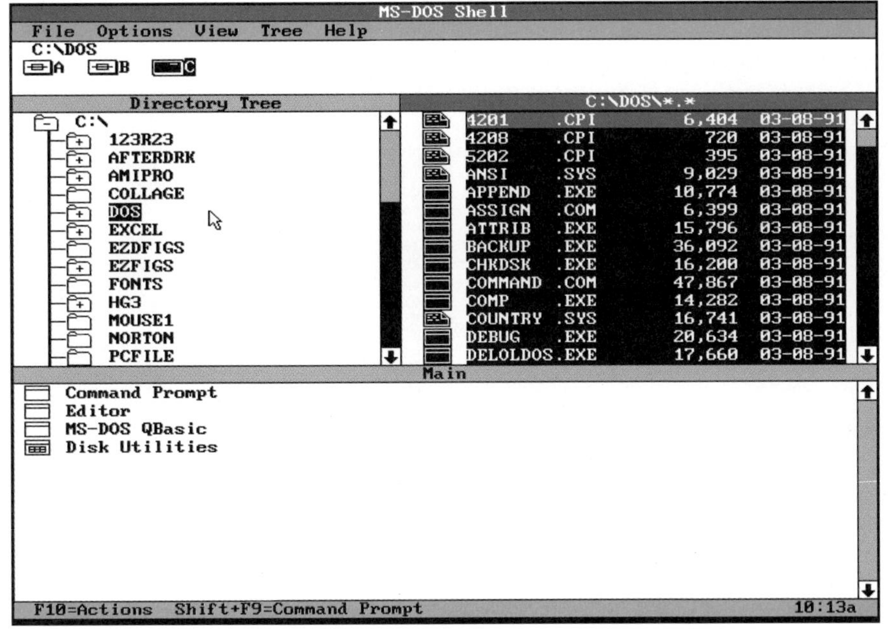

7. Type **S**.

   This step chooses the Select All command. All files in the file list are selected.

   After you highlight the files, you can perform operations on all the selected files. See the other tasks in this section.

Is Select All dimmed?

If the Select All command is dimmed, the command is not available. You probably are not in the file list window. Press the Esc key to close the menu, press Tab to move to the file list window, and then try the command again.

REVIEW

To select all files

1. Start the DOS Shell.
2. If necessary, press **Tab** to move to the Directory Tree window; then select the directory that contains the files you want to select.
3. Press **Tab** to move to the file list window.
4. Press **Alt** to activate the menu bar.
5. Type **F** to open the File menu.
6. Type **S** to select the Select All command.

TASK

Copy a file

before

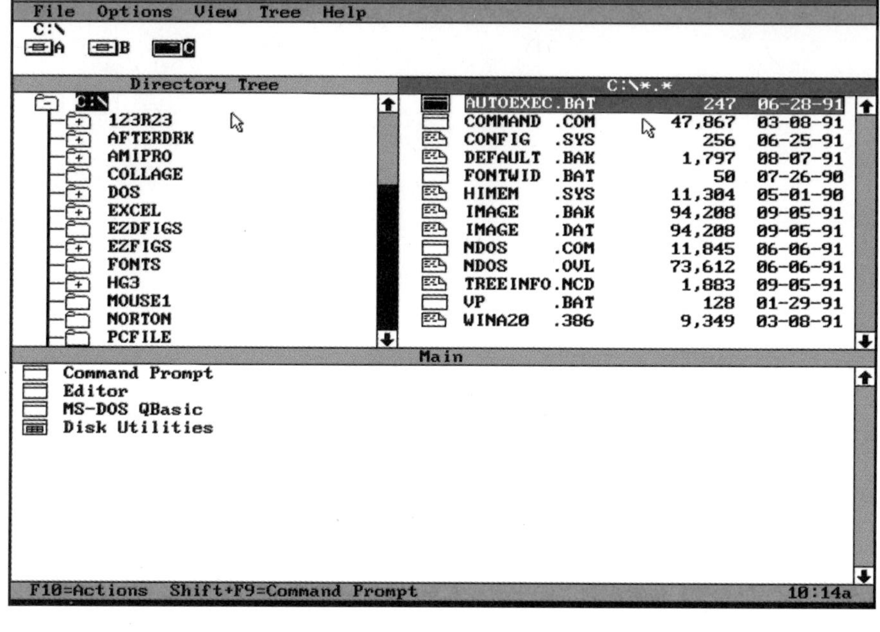

1. Start the DOS Shell.

   For help with this step, see *TASK: Start the DOS Shell.*

2. Press **Tab** until you move to the Directory Tree window.

   This step moves the cursor to the Directory Tree window. The root directory will probably be selected. If it isn't, press ↑ to highlight the root directory.

3. Press **Tab** to move to the file list window.

   You now can select the file you want to copy.

4. Press ↑ or ↓ until you highlight the file AUTOEXEC.BAT.

   AUTOEXEC.BAT is the file that you want to copy. (The Before screen shows this step.)

5. Press **Alt**.

   Pressing the Alt key activates the menu bar.

6. Type **F**.

   This step opens the File menu.

7. Type **C**.

   This step selects the Copy command. On-screen you see the Copy File dialog box. Inside this dialog box you see two text boxes. The cursor is located in the To: box. You type the name of the copy in this box.

Oops!

If you change your mind, press the Esc key in the File Copy dialog box.

after

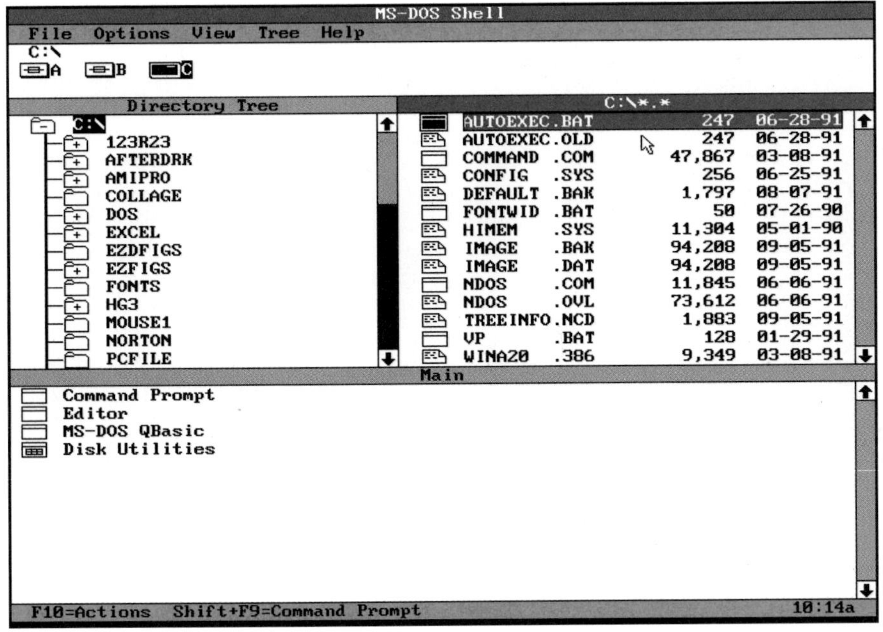

8. Type **AUTOEXEC.OLD**.

   AUTOEXEC.OLD is the name of the file you want to create. You will have two copies of the same file: AUTOEXEC.BAT and AUTOEXEC.OLD.

9. Press **Enter**.

   Pressing Enter confirms the command. The DOS Shell makes a copy of the file. In the directory listing you see the new file.

Try a shortcut

You also can press the F8 key to select the File Copy command.

Note this tip...

When you edit your AUTOEXEC.BAT file, make a copy of the current file. If the new file doesn't work as expected, you can use the copy to return to the original settings.

REVIEW

To copy a file

1. Start the DOS Shell.
2. If necessary, press **Tab** to move to the Directory Tree window; then select the directory that contains the file you want to copy.
3. Press **Tab** to move to the file list window.
4. Use ↑ and ↓ to highlight the file you want to copy.
5. Press **Alt** to activate the menu bar.
6. Type **F** to open the File menu.
7. Type **C** to select the Copy command.
8. Type the name of the new file and press **Enter**.

TASK

Rename a file

before

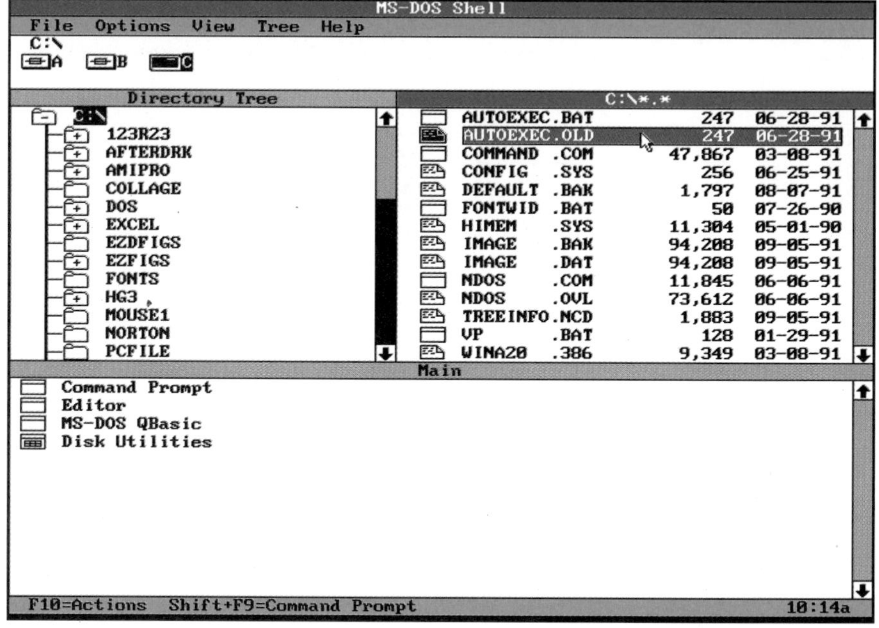

Oops!

Follow this same procedure to return the file to its original name.

1. Start the DOS Shell.

   For help with this step, see *TASK: Start the DOS Shell.*

2. Press **Tab** until you move to the Directory Tree window.

   This step moves the cursor to the Directory Tree window. The root directory will probably be selected. If it isn't, press ↑ to highlight the root directory.

3. Press **Tab** to move to the file list window.

   You now can select the file you want to rename.

4. Press ↓ until you highlight the file AUTOEXEC.OLD.

   AUTOEXEC.OLD is the file that you want to rename. (The Before screen shows this step.)

5. Press **Alt**.

   Pressing the Alt key activates the menu bar.

6. Type **F**.

   This step opens the File menu.

7. Type **n**.

   This step selects the Rename command. On-screen you see the Rename File dialog box. Inside this dialog box you see two text boxes. You type the new name in the New name: text box.

after

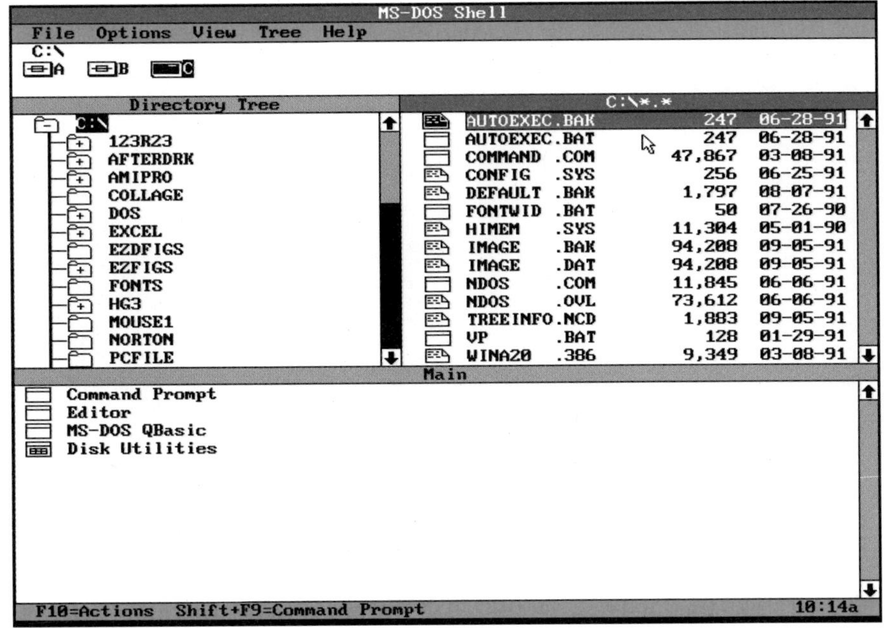

Change your mind?

If you change your mind and don't want to rename the file, press the Esc key in the File Rename dialog box.

8. Type **AUTOEXEC.BAK**.

   AUTOEXEC.BAK is the new file name you want to assign.

9. Press **Enter**.

   Pressing Enter confirms the command. The DOS Shell renames a copy of the file. In the directory listing, you see the file listed with the new name.

REVIEW

To rename a file

1. Start the DOS Shell.
2. If necessary, press **Tab** to move to the Directory Tree window; then select the directory that contains the file you want to rename.
3. Press **Tab** to move to the file list window.
4. Use ↑ or ↓ to highlight the file you want to rename.
5. Press **Alt** to activate the menu bar.
6. Type **F** to open the File menu.
7. Type **n** to select the Rename command.
8. Type the name of the new file and press **Enter**.

File name already exists?

If you type a name that already exists, you see an alert box that tells you access is denied. Type 2 and press Enter to return to the dialog box; then try again.

Move a file

before

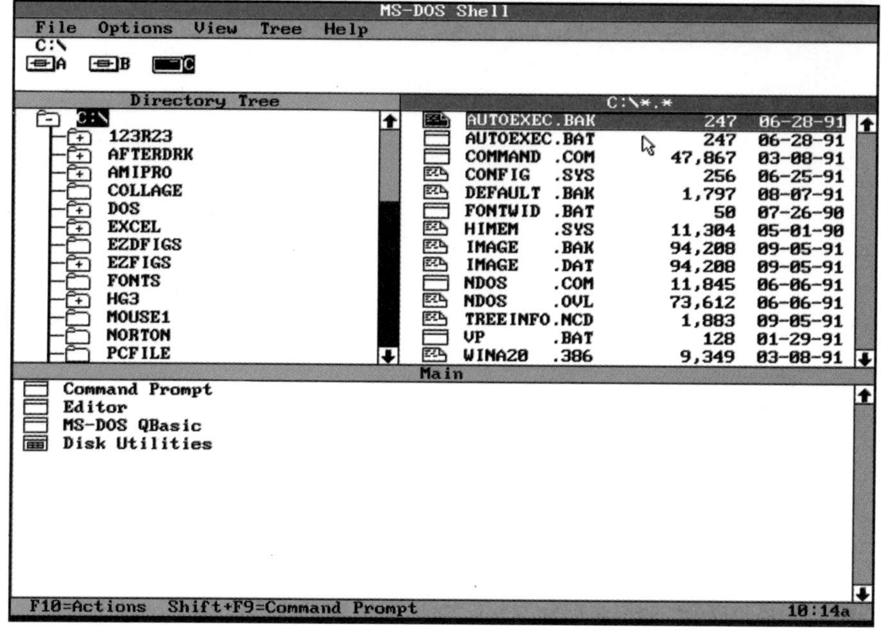

Oops!

If you change your mind and don't want to move the file, press the Esc key in the File Move dialog box.

1. **Start the DOS Shell.**

   For help with this step, see *TASK: Start the DOS Shell.*

2. **Press Tab until you move to the Directory Tree window.**

   This step moves the cursor to the Directory Tree window. The root directory will probably be selected. If it isn't, press ↑ to highlight the root directory.

3. **Press Tab to move to the file list window.**

   You now can select the file you want to move.

4. **Press ↑ or ↓ until you highlight the file AUTOEXEC.BAK.**

   AUTOEXEC.BAK is the file that you want to move. (The Before screen shows this step.)

5. **Press Alt.**

   Pressing the Alt key activates the menu bar.

6. **Type F.**

   This step opens the File menu.

7. **Type M.**

   This step selects the Move command. On-screen you see the Move File dialog box. Inside this dialog box you see two text boxes. You type the new location in the To: box.

after

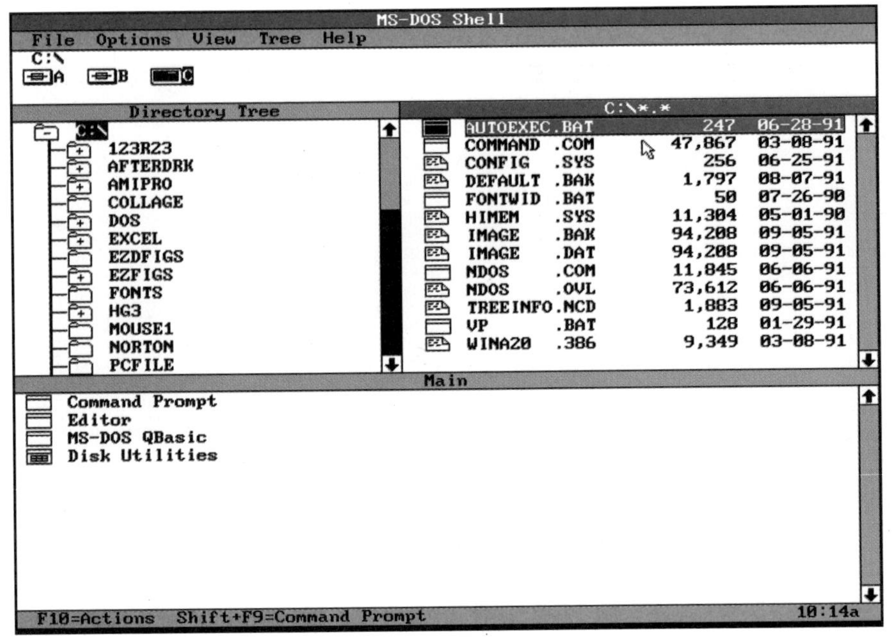

Be careful!

Don't move a file that needs to be in a specific directory. For example, don't move any program files (files with the extension COM, EXE, or BAT).

Try a shortcut

Press F7 to select the File Move command.

8. Type **C:\DOS**.

   C:\DOS is the location where you want to move the file. With this command, you are moving the file to the DOS directory.

9. Press **Enter**.

   Pressing Enter confirms the command. The DOS Shell moves the file. The file entry is moved to the new directory and no longer appears in the current directory listing.

REVIEW

To move a file

1. Start the DOS Shell.
2. If necessary, press **Tab** to move to the Directory Tree window; then select the directory that contains the file you want to move.
3. Press **Tab** to move to the file list window.
4. Use ↑ or ↓ to highlight the file you want to move.
5. Press **Alt** to activate the menu bar.
6. Type **F** to open the File menu.
7. Type **M** to select the Move command.
8. Type the location for the file and press **Enter**.

TASK

Delete a file

before

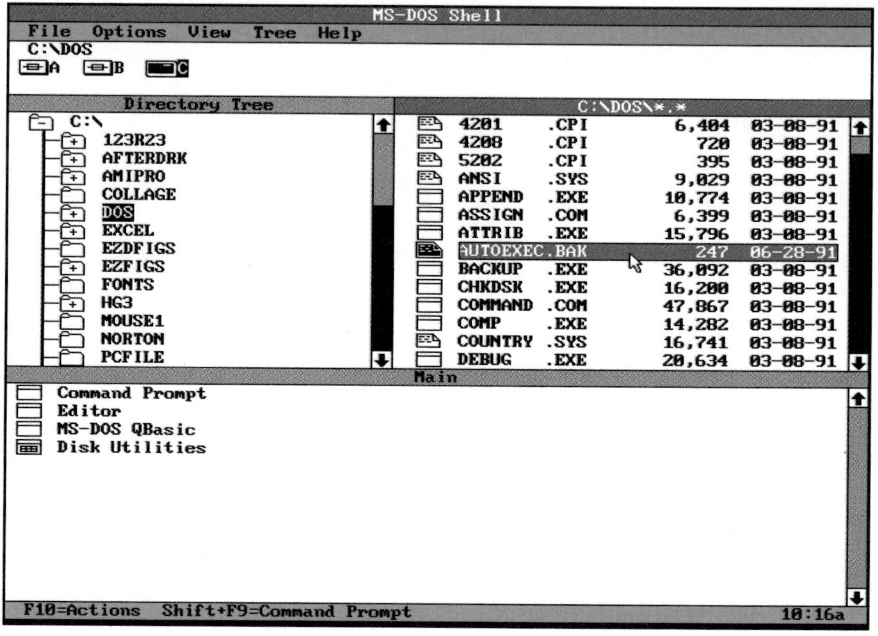

1. Start the DOS Shell.

For help with this step, see *TASK: Start the DOS Shell*. If the DOS Shell is already started, skip this step.

2. Press **Tab** to move to the Directory Tree window.

This step moves the cursor to the Directory Tree window so that you can select the directory.

3. This step selects the DOS directory. If you don't have a directory named DOS, select one that you do have.

4. Press **Tab** to move to the file list window.

This step moves the cursor to the file list window so that you can select the file you want to delete.

5. Press ↑ or ↓ until you highlight the file AUTOEXEC.BAK.

AUTOEXEC.BAK is the file that you want to delete. If you don't have this file, select one you do have. (The Before screen shows this step.) Be sure to select a file that you don't need.

6. Press **Alt**.

Pressing the Alt key activates the menu bar.

7. Type **F**.

This step opens the File menu.

Oops!

If you change your mind and don't want to delete a file, press the Esc key (instead of Enter) in the Delete File Confirmation box.

after

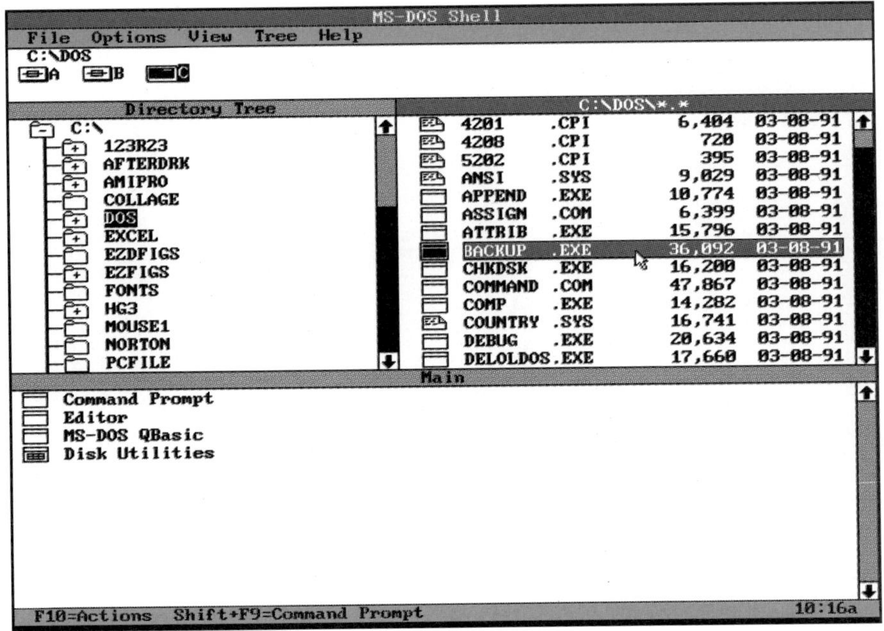

Be careful!

Be sure that you don't delete a file you need. Double-check before you confirm the deletion.

8. Type **D**.

   This step selects the Delete command. On-screen you see the Delete File Confirmation alert box.

9. Press **Enter**.

   Pressing Enter confirms the deletion and deletes the file. The file no longer appears in the current directory listing.

REVIEW

To delete a file

1. Start the DOS Shell.
2. If necessary, press **Tab** to move to the Directory Tree window; then select the directory that contains the file you want to delete.
3. Press **Tab** to move to the file list window.
4. Use ↑ or ↓ to highlight the file you want to delete.
5. Press **Alt** to activate the menu bar.
6. Type **F** to open the File menu.
7. Type **D** to select the Delete command.
8. Press **Enter** to confirm the deletion.

Try a shortcut

You also can press the Del key to select the File Delete command.

View file contents

before

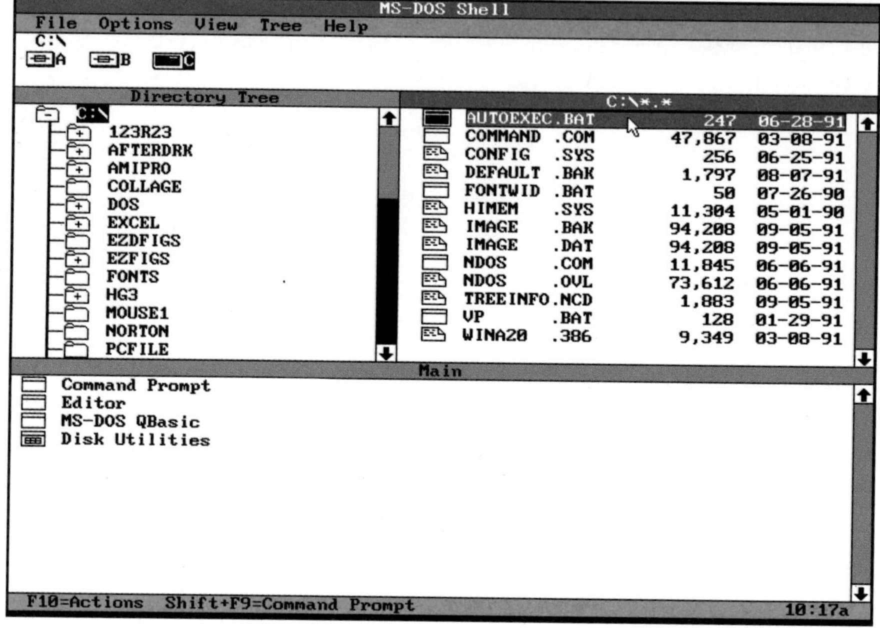

Oops!

Press the Esc key to return to the DOS Shell screen.

1. Start the DOS Shell.

   For help with this step, see *TASK: Start the DOS Shell*. If the DOS Shell is already started, skip this step.

2. Press **Tab** until you move to the Directory Tree window.

   This step moves the cursor to the Directory Tree window. The root directory will probably be selected. If it isn't, press ↑ to highlight the root directory.

3. Press **Tab** to move to the file list window.

   This step moves the cursor to the file list window so that you can select the file you want to display.

4. Press ↑ or ↓ until you highlight the file AUTOEXEC.BAT.

   This step highlights the AUTOEXEC.BAT file, which is the file that you want to display. If you don't have this file, select one you do have. (The Before screen shows this step.)

5. Press **Alt**.

   Pressing the Alt key activates the menu bar.

6. Type **F**.

   Typing F opens the File menu.

after

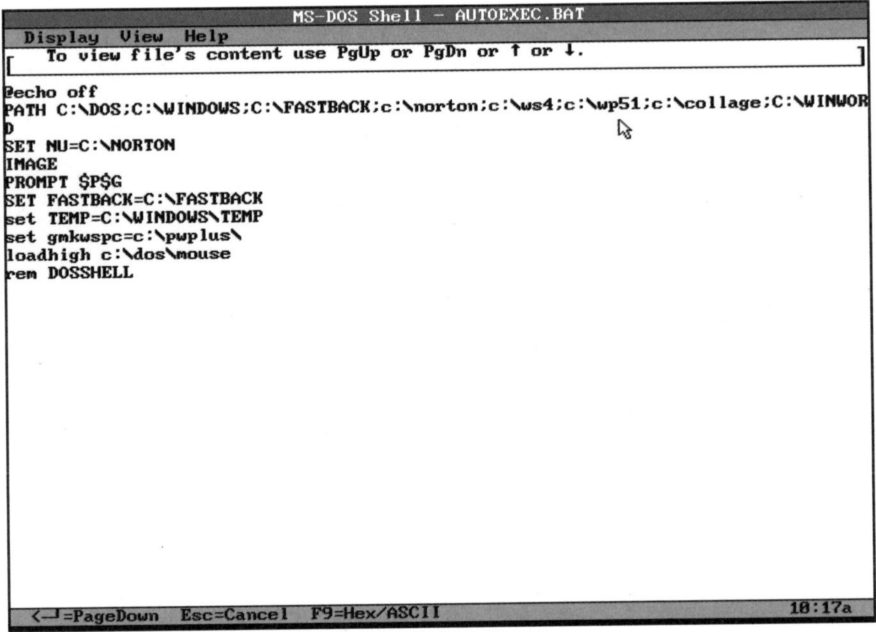
MS-DOS Shell - AUTOEXEC.BAT
Display View Help
To view file's content use PgUp or PgDn or ↑ or ↓.
@echo off
PATH C:\DOS;C:\WINDOWS;C:\FASTBACK;c:\norton;c:\ws4;c:\wp51;c:\collage;C:\WINWOR
D
SET NU=C:\NORTON
IMAGE
PROMPT PG
SET FASTBACK=C:\FASTBACK
set TEMP=C:\WINDOWS\TEMP
set gmkwspc=c:\pwplus\
loadhigh c:\dos\mouse
rem DOSSHELL
<┘=PageDown Esc=Cancel F9=Hex/ASCII
10:17a

7. Type **V**.

   Typing V selects the View File Contents command. On-screen you see the file contents. (What you see may differ from the After screen because your AUTOEXEC.BAT file may contain other commands.)

8. Press **Esc**.

   Pressing the Esc key returns you to the DOS Shell screen.

Do you see a strange display?

Some files (especially program files) contain characters that DOS cannot display. You may see strange characters or many numbers on-screen if you display this type of file. Press the Esc key to stop the display.

REVIEW

To view file contents

1. Start the DOS Shell.
2. If necessary, press **Tab** to move to the Directory Tree window; then select the directory that contains the file you want to display.
3. Press **Tab** to move to the file list window.
4. Use ↑ or ↓ to highlight the file you want to display.
5. Press **Alt** to activate the menu bar.
6. Type **F** to open the File menu.
7. Type **V** to select the View File Contents command.
8. Press **Esc** to quit the display.

Try a shortcut

You also can press the F9 key to select the View File Contents command.

TASK

Search for a file

before

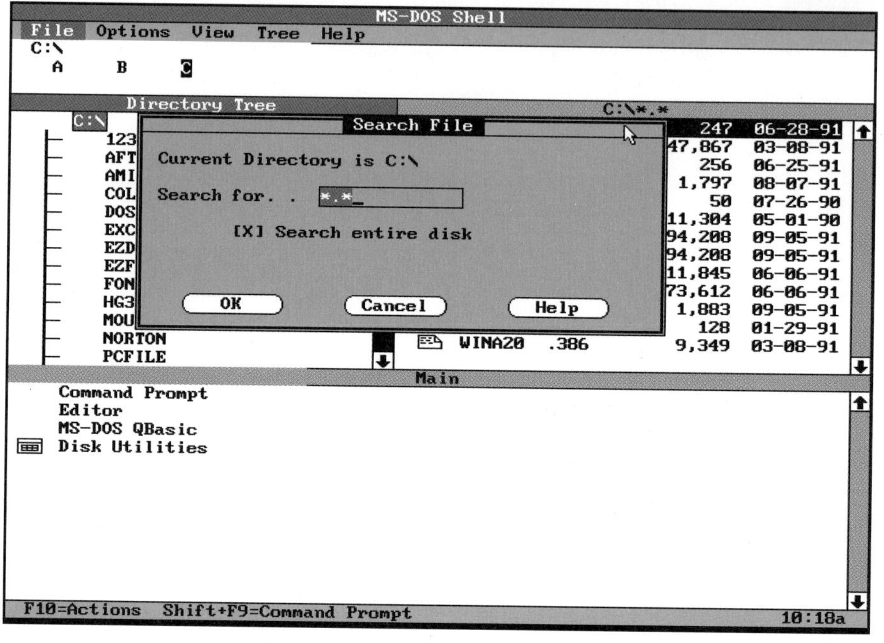

1. **Start the DOS Shell.**

   For help with this step, see *TASK: Start the DOS Shell*. If the DOS Shell is already started, skip this step.

2. **Press Alt.**

   Pressing the Alt key activates the menu bar.

3. **Type F.**

   This step opens the File menu.

4. **Type h.**

   This step selects the Search command. You see the Search File dialog box. The Search for text box contains `*.*`; the cursor is positioned inside this box. Also notice the check box marked `Search entire disk`. When the check box contains an `X`, the DOS Shell looks everywhere on your disk for the file. (The Before screen shows this step.)

5. **Type AUTOEXEC.*.**

   This step tells the DOS Shell to find all files with any extension and the name AUTOEXEC.

Oops!

If the search does not find the requested file, you see the message `No files match file specifier`. Press the Esc key and try the search again. You may have typed the name incorrectly.

after

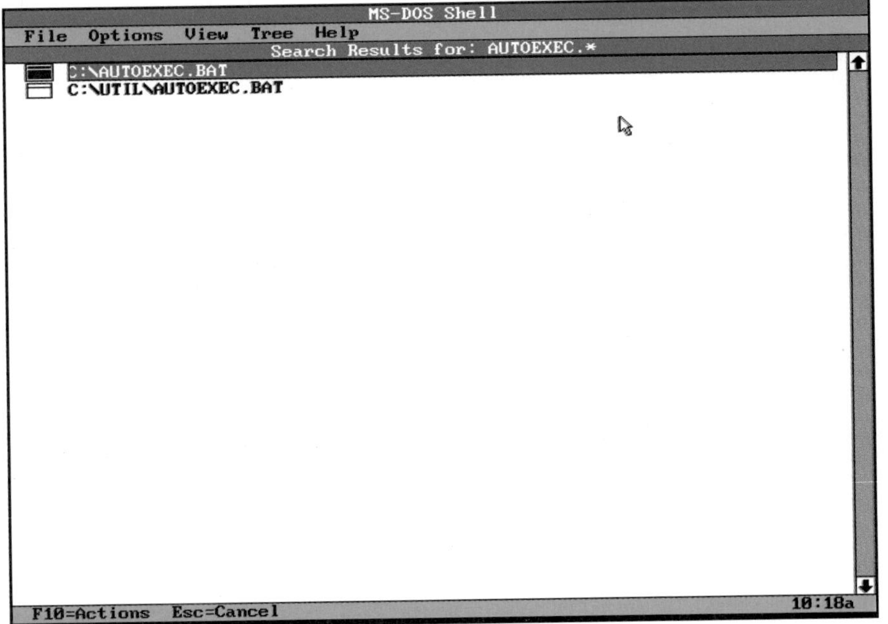

6. Press **Enter**.

   Pressing Enter confirms the name and starts the search. The DOS Shell looks through all directories for files that match this name. When it finds a file, a window appears with the words `Search Results for: AUTOEXEC.*`. You see the location of all matching files.

7. Press **Esc**.

   Pressing the Esc key closes the Search Results window.

What is a wild card?

A wild card is a character that matches any character or characters. The question mark wild card (?) matches a single character. The asterisk wild card (*) matches all characters.

REVIEW

To search for a file

1. Start the DOS Shell.
2. Press **Alt** to activate the menu bar.
3. Type **F** to open the File menu.
4. Type **h** to select the Search command.
5. Type the file name you want to find. You can use wild cards.
6. Press **Enter**.
7. Press **Esc** to close the Search Results window.

Create a directory

before

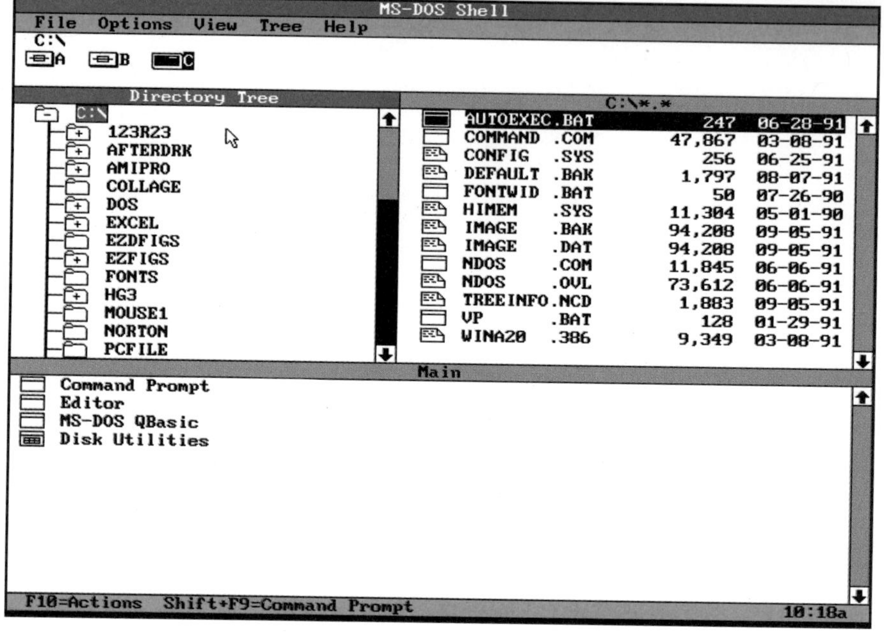

Oops!

Be sure to select the directory that will contain the new directory first. Remember that you are creating the directory within the current directory.

1. Start the DOS Shell.

For help with this step, see *TASK: Start the DOS Shell*. If the DOS Shell is already started, skip this step.

2. Press Tab to move to the Directory Tree window.

This step moves you to the Directory Tree window so that you can create a directory.

3. Be sure that the root directory (C:\) is selected.

You will create a directory that is a subdirectory of the root directory. If you want to place the new directory within another directory, select that directory first.

4. Press Alt.

Pressing the Alt key activates the menu bar.

5. Type F.

This step opens the File menu. You see a list of File commands.

6. Type e.

This step selects the Create Directory command. You see the Create Directory dialog box. This dialog box lists the current directory name (called the Parent name) and contains a New directory name text box.

after

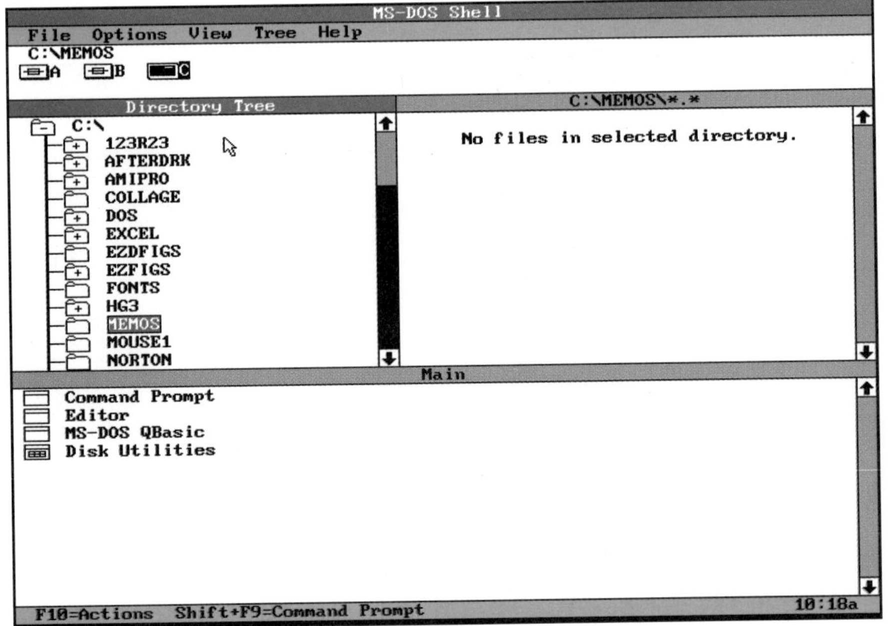

7. Type **MEMOS**.

   MEMOS is the name of the directory that you want to create.

8. Press **Enter**.

   Pressing Enter confirms the name and creates the directory. The new directory is selected. The After screen shows the new directory.

Remove a directory

To remove a directory, see *TASK: Remove a directory*.

Name already exists?

If you type a directory name that already exists, you see a message stating that access is denied. Type **2** and press Enter; then try again. Use a different name this time.

REVIEW

To create a directory

1. Start the DOS Shell.
2. Press **Tab** to move to the Directory Tree window.
3. Use ↑ or ↓ to select the directory that will contain the new directory.
4. Press **Alt** to activate the menu bar.
5. Type **F** to open the File menu.
6. Type **e** to select the Create Directory command.
7. Type the directory name.
8. Press **Enter**.

TASK

Remove a directory

before

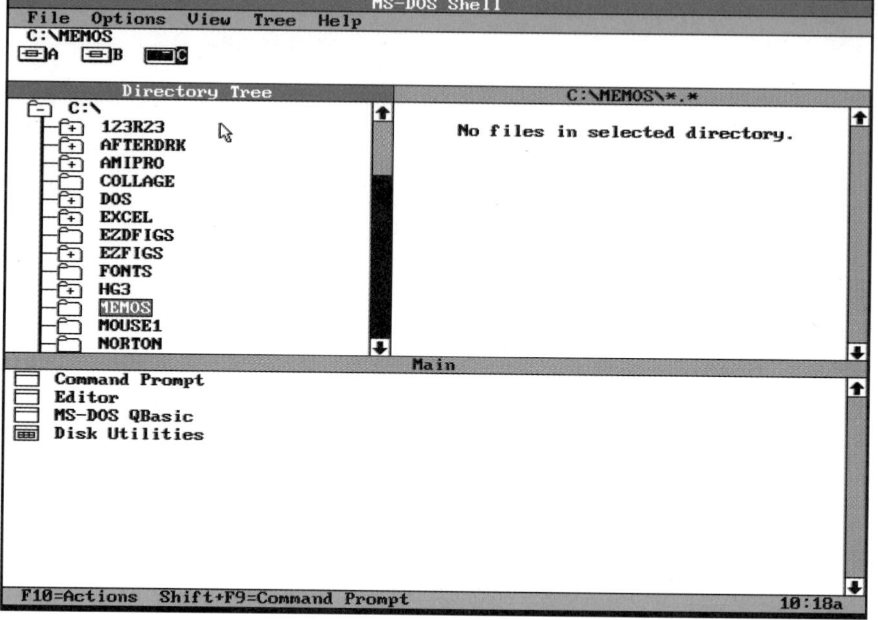

Oops!

If you change your mind and do not want to remove the directory, press the Esc key in the Delete Directory Confirmation box.

1. Start the DOS Shell.

   For help with this step, see *TASK: Start the DOS Shell*. If the DOS Shell is already started, skip this step.

2. Press **Tab** to move to the Directory Tree window.

   This step moves you to the Directory Tree window so that you can remove a directory.

3. Press ↑ or ↓ until you highlight the MEMOS directory.

   MEMOS is the directory that you want to delete. If you don't have this directory, select one that you do have. Be sure to select one that you don't need.

   The MEMOS directory should be empty. If not, you may want to create an empty directory for this exercise. (See *TASK: Create a directory*.) You cannot remove a directory unless all the files in that directory are deleted.

4. Press **Alt**.

   Pressing the Alt key activates the menu bar.

5. Type **F**.

   This step opens the File menu. You see a list of File commands.

after

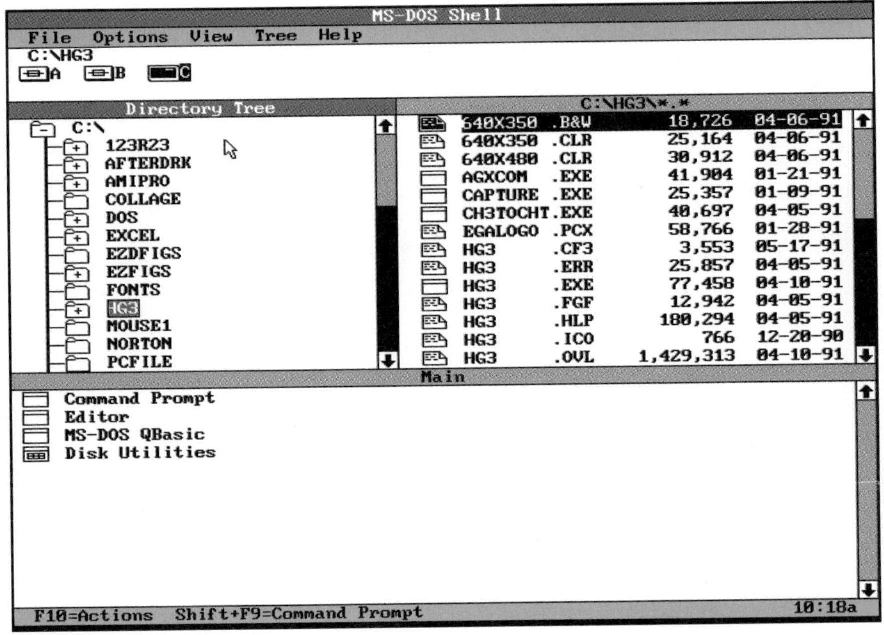

6. Type **D**.

   This step selects the Delete command. You see the Delete Directory Confirmation alert box.

7. Press **Enter**.

   Pressing Enter confirms that you want to delete the directory.

Deletion error

If the directory contains files or other directories, you see a Deletion Error alert box that tells you that you cannot delete a directory that is not empty. Delete all files and subdirectories in the directory and then try again.

REVIEW

To remove a directory

1. Start the DOS Shell.
2. Press **Tab** to move to the Directory Tree window.
3. Use ↑ and ↓ to select the directory that you want to remove.
4. Press **Alt** to activate the menu bar.
5. Type **F** to open the File menu.
6. Type **D** to select the Delete command.
7. Press **Enter** to confirm the deletion.

Reference

Quick Reference

Error Messages

Software Guide

Glossary

Quick Reference

Task	*Command*
Change directories	**CD**
Change the date	**DATE**
Change the time	**TIME**
Change the volume label	**LABEL**
Clear the screen	**CLS**
Copy a disk	**DISKCOPY**
Copy a file	**COPY**
Create a directory	**MD**
Delete a file	**DEL**
Display a directory	**DIR**
Display a file's contents	**TYPE**
Display available disk space	**CHKDSK**
Display available RAM	**MEM** (DOS 5 and 6 only)
Display DOS version	**VER**
Format a disk	**FORMAT**
Remove a directory	**RD**
Rename a file	**RENAME**
Restore files	**RESTORE**
Set the system prompt	**PROMPT**

Error Messages

This guide contains some of the error messages that you might run across and explains what to do when you receive them.

Abort, Retry, Fail?

You might get this message when you are trying to access a disk drive. The message might mean that the disk is not formatted, the disk is bad, or the disk is not inserted properly. Eject and reinsert the disk and try typing **R**. If this doesn't work, type **F** to fail. Or type **A** to abort (cancel) the operation.

You are prompted `Current drive is no longer valid` if you type **F** to fail. Type **C:** and press **Enter** to return to drive C.

All files will be deleted

When you type **DEL *.***, you tell DOS to delete everything in the directory. This command could be dangerous if you don't intend to delete every file in the directory. This message allows you to confirm the deleting (type **Y**) or cancel the command (type **N**).

Bad command or file name

When you type a command that DOS does not recognize, you see the message `Bad command or file name`. You might have simply typed the command incorrectly (such as typing DES instead of DEL). Check your typing and try the command again.

Duplicate file name or file not found

If you used RENAME and typed, as the new name, a name that already exists, you see this message. You also see this message if you used RENAME and typed, as the original file name, a file that doesn't exist. Check the command and try again.

File cannot be copied to itself

If you type the COPY command and don't tell DOS the name of the copy, you receive this error message. Type the command again, but this time specify the name of the file you want to create (the new copy).

File not found

If you try to access a file that is not in the current directory (or not in the path), or if you type the file name incorrectly, you get this message. Check your typing and try again or change to the correct directory and try again.

Insufficient disk space

To copy a file to another disk, that disk must have enough space for the file (or files). If the disk doesn't contain enough space, you get this message. Erase any unneeded files and try again.

Non-System disk or disk error

When DOS starts, it usually looks for certain files. Usually it starts by looking on drive A for these files. If a disk is inserted into drive A, and it is not a system disk (DOS has not been added to it), you see this message. Eject the disk and press any key to continue.

Other Errors

See *Using MS-DOS 6,* Special Edition, for information on other errors you might receive.

Software Guide

To use your computer to perform specific tasks (writing a letter, balancing a budget, storing real estate clients), you need to purchase and install applications. *Applications* are tools you use on the computer. A computer doesn't really perform unless you add different applications (also called *programs* or *software*).

This guide discusses the most common categories of applications, briefly explains what each type does, and lists a few representative software packages. For more information, see *Introduction to Personal Computers,* 3rd Edition, (published by Que) or pick up any personal computing magazine (such as *PC World*, *PCWeek*, *PC Magazine*) and read the ads. If you need help with a particular application, Que publishes titles on most of the popular software packages.

Types of Applications

There are basically 10 categories of applications:

- Word processors
- Spreadsheets
- Databases
- Graphics
- Desktop publishing
- Communication
- Integrated programs
- Financial
- Education
- Games

This software guide discusses each type of category.

A Word about Windows

Microsoft Windows is a graphical user interface. It is designed to be an interface between the user and DOS. (You still need DOS.) Rather than memorize and type commands, you access commands through the menus. Microsoft Windows helps you manage files and run programs.

Some programs are designed specifically to work with Microsoft Windows. These programs work essentially in the same way. That is, after you learn one Windows program, you can easily learn other Windows programs. Some Windows programs are noted in the following sections. To use these programs, you must have Microsoft Windows.

Word Processors

You use word processors to create memos, letters, reports, brochures, and other printed material. A word processor is like a typewriter—but much better.

Most word processors offer several features that let you work with text easily. You can complete these tasks:

See text as you type on-screen. Because the text is not committed to paper, you can make changes and corrections—delete text, add text, and so on.

Rearrange text. As you write, you might decide that the last paragraph really belongs in the introduction. With a word processor, you can move the text from one spot to another. This process is called *cut and paste*.

Spell check your document. Nothing mars a document worse than a glaring typo or misspelled word. Most word processors offer a speller. You can check the spelling of your document before you print.

Save the document. You can save the document on disk and use it again.

Format the document. Word processors vary in the formatting features they offer. Simple word processors enable you to set tabs, change margins, and select different fonts or font styles (bold, italic, and so on). Complex word processors include these features, but they also allow you to add footers and headers, create columns, insert graphics, and so on.

The most common word processing programs are

- Ami Pro (available only for Windows)
- Microsoft Word for DOS
- Microsoft Word for Windows
- Professional Write
- WordPerfect
- WordPerfect for Windows
- WordStar

The following is a screen from Microsoft Word for DOS:

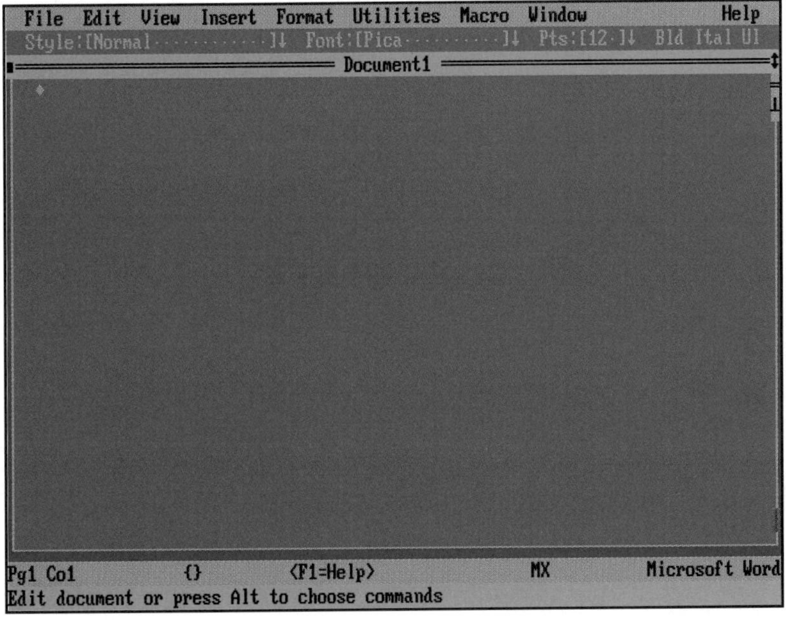

The following is a screen from WordPerfect:

Spreadsheets

A *spreadsheet* is an electronic version of an accountant's pad. You use a spreadsheet program to set up *worksheets*. Worksheets can total sales by division, keep track of a monthly budget, calculate loan balances, and perform other financial analysis.

With a spreadsheet program, you can complete these tasks:

Calculate formulas. You can write simple formulas to add, subtract, multiply, and divide. You can depend on the spreadsheet program to calculate the results correctly every time.

Change data and recalculate. You can change, add, or delete data, and then recalculate the results automatically. You never have to erase and rewrite when you forget a crucial figure. And you don't have to recalculate all the amounts manually when you do make a change or an addition.

Rearrange data. With your worksheet on-screen, you can add or delete a column or row. You can copy and move data from one spot to another.

Repeat information. You can copy text, a value, or a formula to another place in the worksheet. In your monthly budget worksheet, for example, you total the expenses for each month. You could write a formula that calculates January's totals, and you then could copy this formula for February through December.

Change the format of data. You can format your results in many ways. You can display a number with dollar signs, as a percent, or as a date. You can align text left, right, or center.

Print data. You can print reports of your data.

Create charts. Most spreadsheet programs allow you to graph your data and print that graph. You can create pie graphs, bar graphs, line graphs, and many other graph types.

The most common spreadsheet programs are

- Lotus 1-2-3
- Microsoft Excel (available for Windows)
- Quattro Pro

The following is a screen from Lotus 1-2-3:

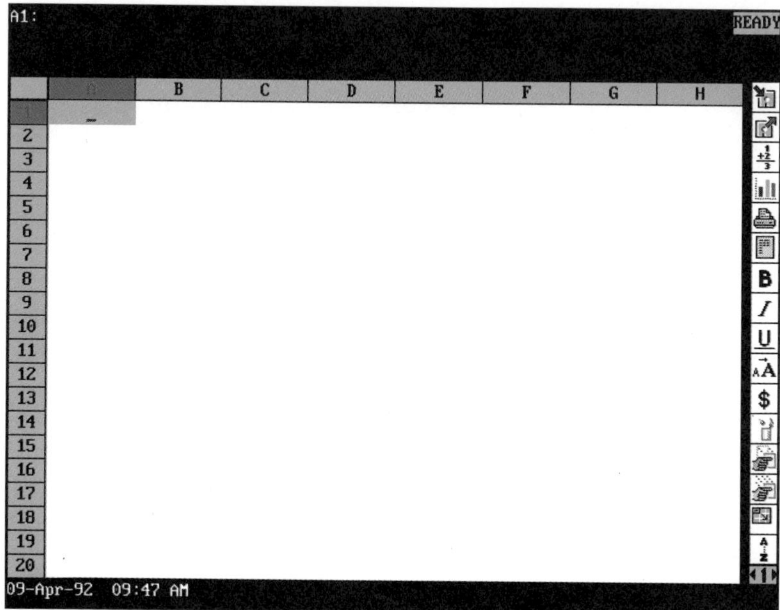

The following is a screen from Quattro Pro:

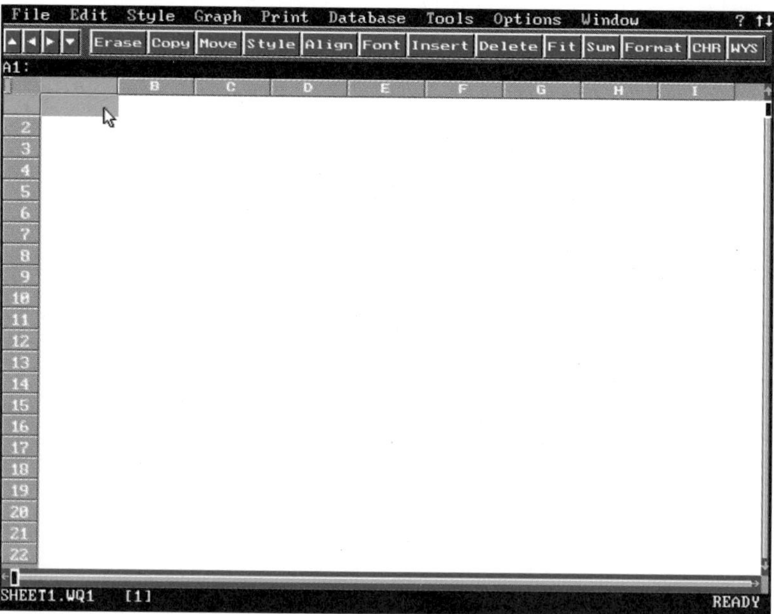

Databases

A *database* is similar to a complex card file. You store related information together. For example, you can use a database to keep track of real estate clients, a baseball card collection, employees, inventory—any set of data.

Each piece of data, such as a phone number, is stored in a *field*. A set of fields makes up a *record*, such as a name, address, and phone number. A *database* is a collection of all the records.

With a database, you can complete these tasks:

Retrieve data. After you enter data, you can retrieve it easily. Rather than sift through several paper documents, you can quickly pull up the data on-screen—for instance, an invoice.

Sort data. You can rearrange data. For example, you might want an alphabetical list of clients sorted by last name to use as a phone list. You might want to sort the same list by ZIP code to do a mailing.

Print data. You can print reports, mailing labels, and other output.

Some of the most common database packages include

- dBASE
- Paradox
- Personal R:BASE
- Q&A

The following is a screen from Q&A:

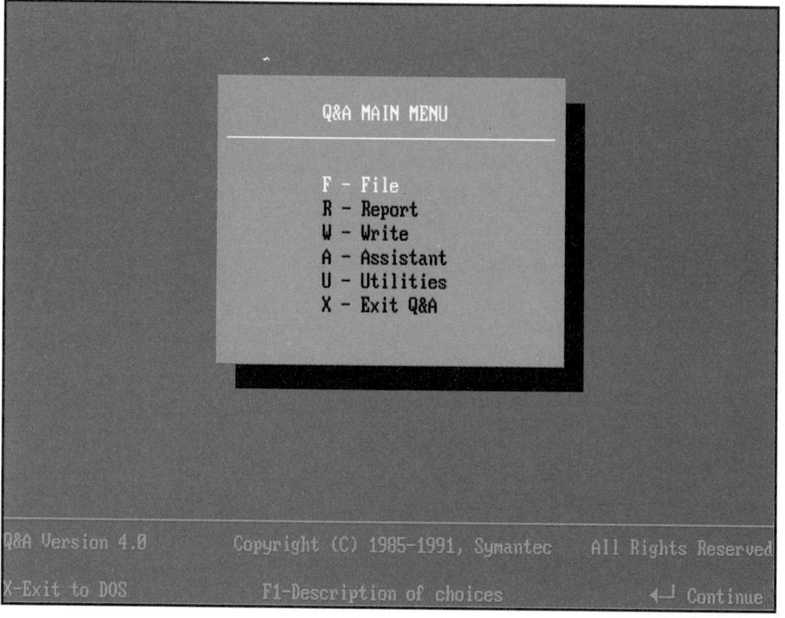

Graphics

With graphics programs, you can create simple to complex illustrations. This category also includes presentation programs, which enable you to create graphs, and computer-aided design (CAD) programs, which enable you to create architectural and other complex drawings.

With graphics programs, you can do the following:

Use many drawing tools. The tools offered by packages vary. You can draw geometric shapes (such as circles, squares, rectangles, and lines), add fills and color, add text, trace objects, align objects, and so on.

Edit drawings. If you don't get the drawing just right, you can modify it. You can delete parts of the drawing and redraw them.

Create drawings to be used over and over. You might, for instance, create a logo that you can use on hundreds of company documents.

Programs in this category include

- AutoCAD (CAD)
- CorelDRAW! (draw)
- Generic CAD (CAD)
- Harvard Graphics (presentation)
- PC Paintbrush (draw)
- PowerPoint (charts; available for Windows)

The following is a screen from PC Paintbrush:

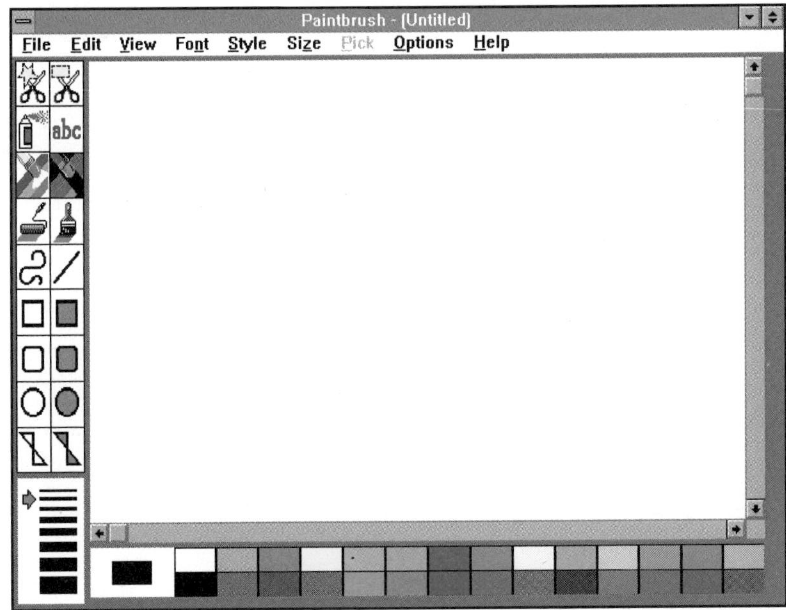

The following is a screen from Harvard Graphics:

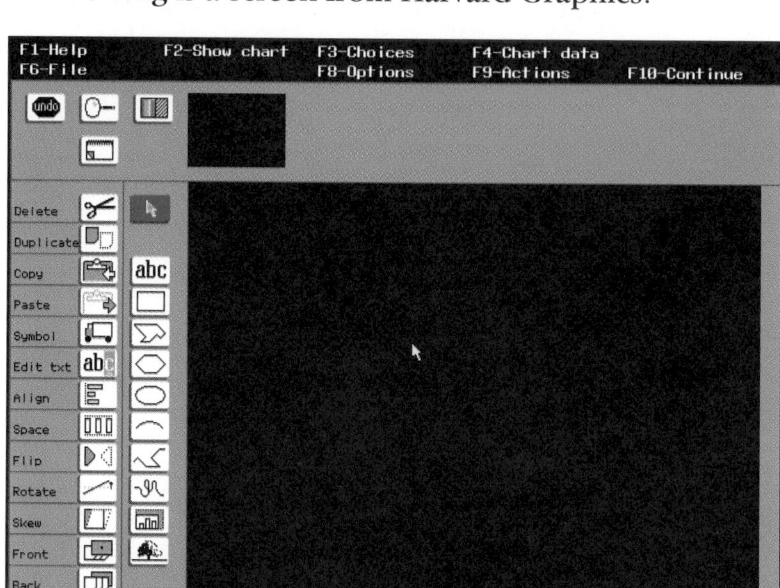

Desktop Publishing

Desktop publishing programs enable you to create sophisticated brochures, newsletters, fliers, resumes, menus, reports, and other output. Some word processing packages offer desktop publishing capabilities (such as column layout), but the features offered by desktop publishing programs are more sophisticated. Keep in mind that if you do use a desktop publishing program, you also will probably use a word processor to create the text.

With a desktop publishing program, you can complete the following tasks:

Lay out a page. With a desktop publishing program, you have precise control over the layout of the page—the margins, headers, footers, and so on. You also have control over the text—what font, size, and style are used; where the text is placed; and how the text flows.

Change page layout. If you don't like how the document looks, you can experiment with the layout until you get the document just the way you want it.

Create templates. You can create a template for a document that you create over and over—such as a newsletter. The headings and layout would be set—you just have to add the text.

The most popular desktop publishing packages are

- Microsoft Publisher
- PageMaker
- PFS: First Publisher
- Ventura Publisher

The following is a screen from Ventura Publisher:

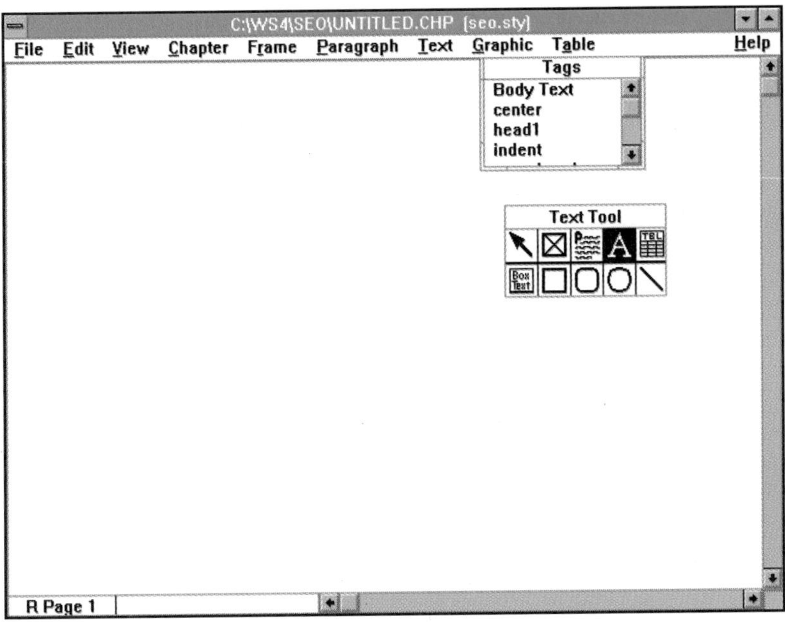

Communication

Communication programs enable you to use your computer to talk to other computers. You might, for example, need to access a huge computer (called a *mainframe*) that stores stock figures so that you can get up-to-the-minute reports. Or you might need some sales data from your district office's computer. With a communication program, you can send and receive information over the phone lines.

You also can connect to on-line services (such as GEnie or CompuServe) that enable you to shop, leave messages for other users, play games with other users (even users in other countries!), download programs, and so on.

To use your computer to communicate, you must also have a modem and a phone line. (For more information on modems, see *Introduction to Personal Computers,* 3rd Edition, or *Introduction to PC Communication*, published by Que.) You also need a communication package. PROCOMM PLUS is an example of this type of package.

Integrated Programs

Integrated programs combine several types of programs into one package: word processing, database, spreadsheet, and communications. Each program offers the benefits previously discussed. Integrated programs also have the added benefit of allowing you to integrate the data from one program to the next. For example, you can use the mailing list from your database to personalize form letters with your word processor. You can copy financial figures from the spreadsheet to a report in the word processor. On the downside, each of the programs will not offer as many features as "stand-alone" or dedicated packages.

Here are some examples of this type of program:

- LotusWorks
- Microsoft Works
- PFS: WindowWorks (available for Windows)
- PFS:First Choice

The following is a screen from Microsoft Works:

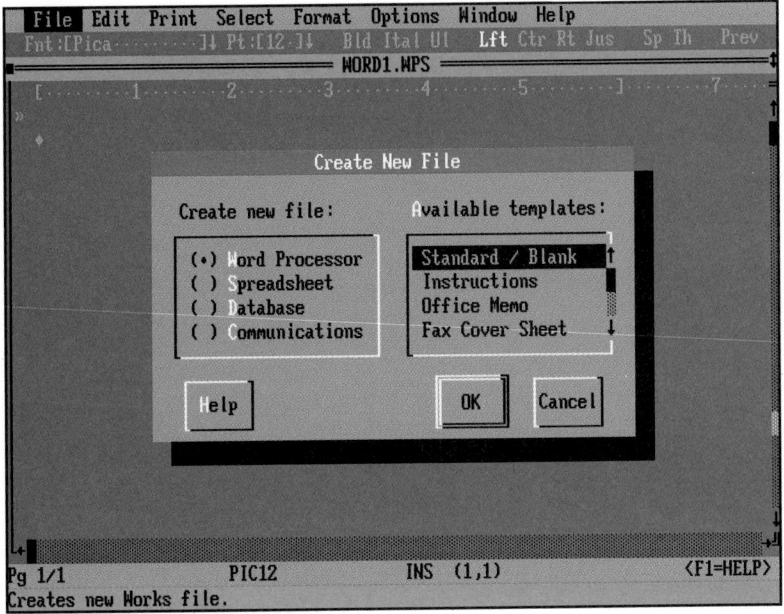

Financial Programs

Financial programs enable you to create tax returns, balance your checkbook, set up an accounting system, and perform other finance-related tasks. These programs range from the simple to the complex. Some examples are

- Peachtree (complete accounting package—general ledger, accounts receivable, accounts payable, payroll)
- Quicken (simple check-writing program; also can be used for limited accounting purposes)
- TurboTax (tax preparation program)

The following is a screen from Quicken:

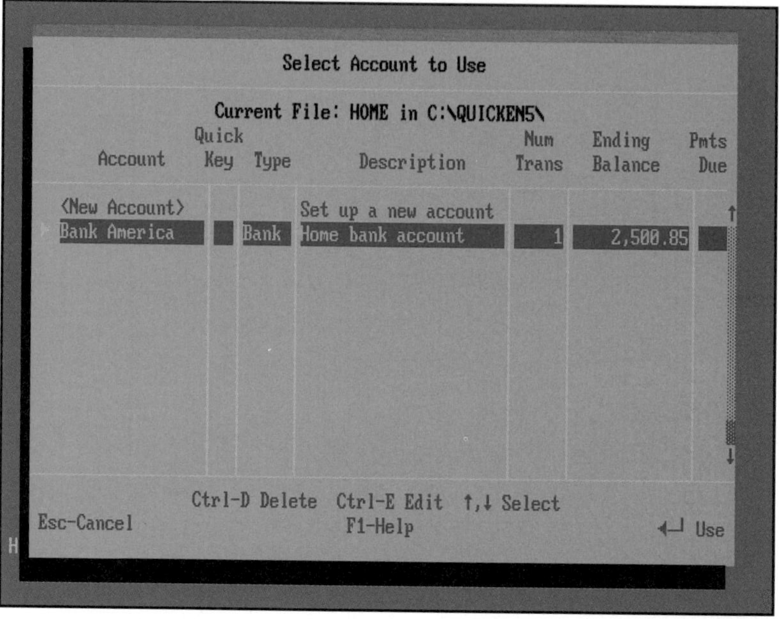

Education

Personal computers are easy to use, which makes them ideal for learning new tasks. You can use programs to learn to type, master a foreign language, plan a travel route for a trip, and accomplish many other educational tasks.

Games

Last but not least, you can use the computer to play games. Games can range from playing on-screen card games (Solitaire) to diagnosing and performing surgery on a patient (Life and Death) to playing golf (Mean 18 Ultimate Golf) to flying a plane (Flight Simulator).

The following is a screen from Solitaire:

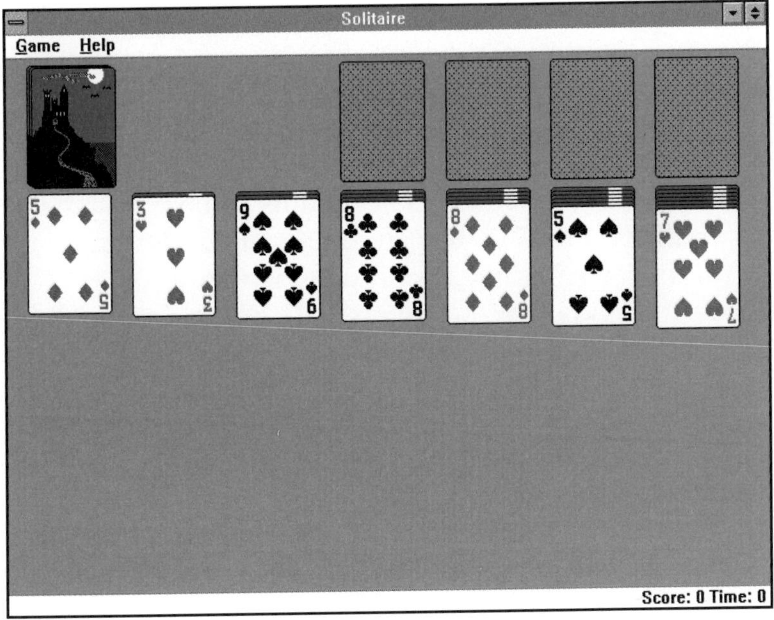

Others

Not all programs fit into a neat category. New programs are created every day. Programs are available that enable you to draw up a will, create a calendar, complete complex statistical analyses, and calculate calories. Just browse through some of the computer magazines (*PC World* or *PC Week*, for example) to get an idea of the world of possibilities. Explore with your computer. Be productive. But most of all, have fun.

Glossary

application A computer program used for a particular task—such as word processing. In most cases, *program*, *software*, and *application* mean the same thing and can be used interchangeably.

AUTOEXEC.BAT A file that DOS executes when you start the computer. This file may include commands that control different settings. You might, for example, include a PATH command that tells DOS where your programs are located.

backup A copy of data or programs that you make in case the original data or program becomes damaged.

batch file A file that contains a series of DOS commands. The commands are executed when you run the batch file. You might create a batch file that changes to a certain directory and starts a program, for example.

boot The process of starting a computer.

byte A measure of the amount of information that is equal to about one character.

capacity A term used to describe how much data you can store on a disk. Capacity is measured in kilobytes (K) or megabytes (M).

COMMAND.COM An essential DOS file that contains the command processor.

CONFIG.SYS A special file that sets configuration settings. DOS consults this file when started. Some applications require that special commands be in the CONFIG.SYS file.

cursor A marker used to indicate the current position on-screen.

defragment A method of rearranging the information on your hard disk so that files are stored in contiguous sections. Defragmenting a disk can improve (speed up) the performance of the disk.

density A term used to describe the amount of information you can store on a floppy disk. Double-density disks store 360 kilobytes or 720 kilobytes of data; high-density disks store 1.2 megabytes or 1.44 megabytes of data.

directory An index to the files stored on disk or a list of files. A directory is similar to a file cabinet; you can group files together in directories.

DOS Acronym for *disk operating system*. DOS manages the details of your system—storing and retrieving programs and files.

DOS prompt The indicator you see on-screen (for instance, `C:>`) that tells you DOS is ready for a command.

file The various individual reports, memos, databases, and letters that you store on your hard drive (or floppy disk) for future use.

file name The name you assign a file when you store it to disk. A file name consists of two parts: the root and the extension. The root can be up to eight characters in length. The extension can be up to three characters long and usually indicates the file type. The root and extension are separated by a period. SALES.DOC is a valid file name. SALES is the root, and DOC is the extension.

file spec The combination of file name and extension, usually with the use of wild cards. The file spec *.DOC means all files with the DOC extension. The file spec MEMO.* means all files named MEMO with any extension.

floppy disk A storage device. Floppy disks come in two sizes (3 1/2-inch and 5 1/4-inch), two densities (double-density and high-density), and different capacities. (5 1/4-inch disks can store either 360 kilobytes or 1.2 megabytes. 3 1/2-inch disks can store either 720 kilobytes or 1.44 megabytes.)

floppy disk drive A device that reads (retrieves) and writes (stores) information on a floppy disk.

format The process that prepares a disk for use.

hard disk A data storage device. Hard disks vary in size—they can range from 20 megabytes to over 155 megabytes. They also vary in type. Some hard disks are encased in the system unit. You also can have an external hard disk that is outside the system unit.

hardware The physical parts of the computer—the screen, the keyboard, the mouse, and so on.

kilobyte (K) About one thousand (1,024) bytes. Kilobytes measure disk capacity.

megabyte (M) One million bytes of information. Megabytes measure disk capacity.

monitor The piece of hardware that displays on-screen what you type on the keyboard.

mouse A pointing device used in some programs to move the mouse pointer on-screen, select windows, and issue commands.

path The route, through directories, to a program or document file. The path C:\REPORTS\SALES\EASTDIV.DOC, for example, includes five elements: the disk drive (C:); the root directory (\); the directory (REPORTS); the subdirectory, which is a directory within the first directory (SALES); and the file name (EASTDIV.DOC).

program A set of instructions that tells a computer what to do. *Program* means the same as *application* or *software*.

RAM An acronym for *random-access memory*. A temporary place where the computer stores data and program instructions.

restore The procedure used to copy backup files back to the hard disk. Because backup files are stored in a special format, you must use a special restore program to restore the files to their original format.

root directory The main directory. All other directories branch off the root directory.

shell A program that acts as a user interface to the features of an operating system.

software Another term for computer programs or applications. You run software on your hardware.

subdirectory A list of files or an index to the files stored on disk. A directory is similar to a file cabinet; you can group files together in directories. *Subdirectory* means the same as *directory*.

syntax The format and rules you follow when issuing a command.

virus A program that carries out unwanted and sometimes damaging procedures on your computer.

wild card A character used to represent other characters. A question mark (?) wild card matches any single character. An asterisk (*) wild card matches any number of characters.

Index

D

E

F

G

H

I-J

K

N

O

P

T

U

V

W-Z